Short Stories of

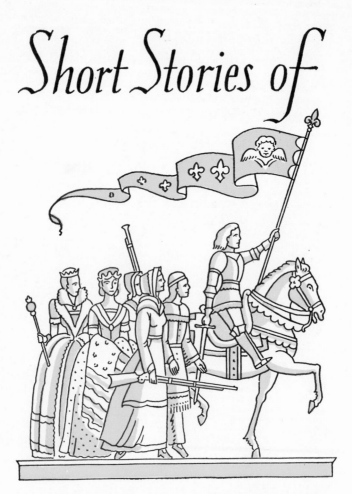

ILLUSTRATED BY VALENTI ANGELO

FAMOUS WOMEN

Edited by PEARL A. WANAMAKER

Superintendent of Public Instruction, State of Washington

NOBLE & NOBLE, PUBLISHERS, Inc.
NEW YORK

PREFACE

This supplementary reader is a companion book to the popular Reynolds' *Short Stories of Famous Men*. Since that book was first published, there has been an ever-increasing demand from the schools for a companion book. It has been suggested that due credit should be given the women of America for their magnificent part in developing the United States into the great nation that it is today. The book should also provide exciting stories that would inspire the boys as well as the girls.

It seems strange that in the various history textbooks in common use in the schools today the names of so few women are mentioned. In order to correct this omission, this book was written to correlate with the history texts and to show some of the ways in which women have helped to develop our American way of life.

It is impossible, of course, to include the names of all the women who have become famous. However, as a basis for the selection of the stories that have been included, the records of America's Hall of Fame at New York University, the National Education Association, the American Library Association, The Daughters of the Revolution, the United Daughters of the Confederacy, State Historians, the General Federation of Women's Clubs, and other similar organizations have been consulted. The history texts in use in the schools have been examined, and the various commemorative stamps issued by the United States Government honoring famous women have been taken into consideration.

Each story is a thrilling and dramatic narrative of a girl who has become famous. It has been said that truth is stranger than fiction. This is a collection of true stories. The principal dates and events have been checked with at least five or more authoritative source books for accuracy.

CONTENTS

vii

IN WAR AND PEACE

ON STAGE!

FAMOUS EDUCATORS

RECENT TIMES

INTRODUCTION

CORNELIA

From the ancient days of the Egyptians, the Greeks, and the Romans, to the present day, women have played such an important part in making history that it seems strange that so few names of women appear in the history textbooks. Perhaps it is because in days gone by most women stayed in the background and were happy and content to let the world praise their husbands or their sons.

There is the famous old Roman story of *Cornelia and Her Jewels*. When her husband died, Cornelia was left without very much money, but she did not care. She was happy that she had such fine children and devoted her life to educating them to become useful citizens. Although a widow, Cornelia was still young and beautiful. Many men, including the King of Egypt, wanted to marry her, but she refused them so that she could spend her time with her children.

One day a wealthy lady came to call and proudly showed the valuable jewels she was wearing. Then she turned to Cornelia and said, "Now you must show me your jewels."

Cornelia was not ashamed that she had no gold rings or expensive necklaces. She called her two sons to her side, and, putting her arms lovingly about them, she said, "These are my only jewels, but they are worth more to me than all the riches on earth."

Thanks to the fine training they had received from their mother, these two boys, known as the Gracchi, did become great men in Rome.

"Now you must show me your jewels."

Everyone has read about George Washington, the "Father of our Country." But what about his wife, Martha, who shared his joys and sorrows? Each year when the American army went into winter quarters during the War of Independence, Martha Washington joined the General and helped him in every way she could. During the terrible, bitter winter of 1777-1778, while the ragged and discouraged American army was encamped at Valley Forge near Philadelphia, Martha gathered the wives of the officers around her. These good ladies did everything they could to relieve the sufferings of the soldiers. They knitted stockings and mittens for the half frozen men. They might be called the first American Red Cross group.

You will not find in the history textbooks any mention of Abigail Adams, and yet she was the "First Lady" to occupy the White House in Washington, D. C.

Furthermore, she is the only woman in the history of our country who was the wife of one President, John Adams, and the mother of another, John Quincy Adams.

During the Revolutionary War, Abigail Adams gave to the patriotic Minute Men of Massachusetts the pewter spoons from her table and helped them melt the spoons in her kitchen to make bullets that were fired in the Battle of Bunker Hill.

Abigail believed in giving women some of the rights and opportunities that were at that time open only to men. When her husband was attending the Continental Congress in Philadelphia, she wrote him, "I desire you would remember the ladies and be more generous and favorable to them than were your ancestors."

In those early days women were content to let their husbands and sons have all the glory. In fact, there was not much opportunity for women to do the many things that are open to them today. It was only after many years of hard work and planning that women were able to win equal rights with men.

Leaders like Susan B. Anthony, Lucretia Mott, Elizabeth Cady Stanton, Anna Howard Shaw, Carrie Chapman Catt, and many others fought for the right of women to vote so that women could have an opportunity to help choose the persons who make the laws to govern the country.

The women of today owe a great deal to those who fought their battles amid the boos and jeers of the crowds. In later life Susan B. Anthony stood on a platform and spoke about the justice of giving women the right to vote.

After she had finished, the men and women in the audience rose and cheered her for all the fine things she had done to help women gain their rights. Many threw roses at her feet as a tribute to her courage and hard work.

"Time brings strange changes," said Susan Anthony with a smile. "In this very city that has pelted me with roses, I have been pelted with rotten eggs for saying the very things that I have said tonight."

Yes, time does bring many changes. To-day we find in the United States over three million girls in public high schools and more than a half million young women in college, studying subjects that were unknown to their grandmothers.

Within recent years women have been appointed as Ambassadors of the United States to foreign countries; they have sat in the Cabinet advising Presidents; they have been elected as United States Senators and Governors of states. In fact, they have occupied nearly every kind of important position in the nation. In almost every kind of business today you will find women working side by side with men in every important type of work. This is the American way of life.

In the pages of this book are the stories of some of the brave and talented girls and women who have won fame. Many of them have helped to fight for freedom and democracy; others have helped to build our nation. Some have fought for the rights of women. Others have worked for better living conditions for everyone, regardless of his or her race, color, or creed. Still others have gained fame through their own brilliant achievements in science, in literature, and in nearly every other type of work. Thus by their tireless efforts they have paved the way and opened the door of opportunity for any woman to gain happiness and success in any field of work. The stories of the lives of these famous women will serve as an inspiration to everyone.

xvi

SHORT STORIES
OF
FAMOUS WOMEN

THE GIRL
WHO SAVED FRANCE

JOAN OF ARC

"Your Majesty, I have been sent to you
by the King of Heaven to save our beloved
land and to crown you King of France."

Charles was indeed surprised when he
heard these words from the 17-year-old
maiden who kneeled before him. How
could this young girl drive out the English
who had defeated the great army of France
at the Battle of Agincourt, and who were
now in control of much of his country?
Yet he knew that many Frenchmen believed in the legend that some day a maid
would come to save the nation.

"Arise, Joan of Arc!" he said. "If the
King of Heaven has sent you, indeed you

shall lead my armies to victory. Vive la France!"

Fourteen years before that day, King Henry of England had crossed the channel and had invaded France with 15,000 soldiers, most of whom were armed only with bows and arrows. The French knights and nobles had quickly assembled to repel the invasion.

Soon they had gathered an army together four times as large as that of the English. In their shiny, heavy armor they rode forward, sure of victory. However, the French knights were so weighed down with their heavy armor that they were no match for the lightly clad British, who let fly a cloud of arrows into the advancing ranks of the knights. Most of the French nobles died on the field of battle that day.

Not far away in the little town of Domremy, a 3-year-old peasant girl was out playing with her brothers and sisters in the fields near the cottage of her father, Monsieur d'Arc. Her name was Jeanne d'Arc or, as we would say, Joan of Arc. No one would have thought that fifteen years later the little girl would defeat the British at Orleans and crown Charles King of France.

Joan never went to school and was not even taught how to read and write, but she went to the near-by church on Sunday and loved to listen to the stories of the saints.

One day when she was 12 years old, she thought that she heard one of the angels calling to her from Heaven. After that she often heard the angel voices telling her to leave her home to go to the aid of France. By the time she was 17, she felt sure that, with the help of these angels, she could save France.

Finally she went to see Robert de Baudricourt, the lord of the village of Domremy, to ask for men and weapons. At first he laughed at her for daring to come to him for help. How could a poor farm girl who knew nothing about fighting expect to save France? He was ready to send her home.

But the people who had gathered to listen to her story believed her. They were sure that she had been talking to the angels. They gave her a horse and offered to go with her to see Charles, who was then at his castle at Chinon. And so Joan of Arc, dressed as a young knight, at the head of a small band of armed men, rode away to offer her services to save France.

Charles believed, too, that with divine help this maid might turn back the English invaders, so he made her commander in chief of his army. At that time the city of Orleans was under attack by the English. Joan of Arc, at the head of 8,000 men who were fired by her courage and enthusiasm, set off to rescue the city. She was clad in

4

Joan of Arc set off to rescue Orleans.

snow-white armor and rode a handsome black horse. A sword hung at her side, and, in her left hand, she carried a white banner with angels painted upon it to show that she was going forward with divine help.

Joan of Arc sent a note to the British attacking Orleans calling upon them in the name of the King of Heaven to depart. This they refused to do. After ten days of bitter fighting, the British fled, and Joan of Arc, at the head of her victorious army, entered the city. There, amid the shouts of the people, she was welcomed as a saint.

But Joan did not stay long in Orleans. She had promised to crown Charles King of France in Rheims where Clovis, the first Christian King of France, had been crowned 900 years before. She met Charles at Tours, and together, at the head of the army, they rode toward Rheims. The English fled before them. At last, the victorious

French arrived at the cathedral city. July 17, 1429, was a great day for France when the crown was placed on Charles' head and he became King.

Joan of Arc believed that her work was now over, and she begged to be allowed to return home. But Charles refused to let her go as he wanted her to continue the fight against the British until they were driven out of the country. In leading the attack on Paris, Joan of Arc was badly wounded and fell into the hands of the Burgundians, who sold her to the British. Because the French people adored Joan of Arc and were willing to follow her so courageously into battle, the British wanted to get rid of her. They were determined that she must die. She was, therefore, brought to trial as a witch and sentenced to be burned at the stake.

Joan of Arc denied that she was a witch or that she had anything to do with the devil. As the flames rose about her, she cried to the ten thousand persons there in the square at Rouen, "It was God who sent me. Now I am going back to Him."

The daring deeds of this "Maid of Orleans," spurred on by her belief that right makes might, have been an inspiration for everyone. Many statues have been erected in her honor. Many stories and plays have been written about her, and countless millions of girls have dreamed that they, like Joan of Arc, might someday lead their country to victory.

QUEEN ISABELLA

"What has happened to Christopher Columbus, Sire?" said Queen Isabella to her husband, King Ferdinand. "I have not seen him for many days."

It was January, 1492, and a cold wind swept through the palace at Granada. King Ferdinand pulled his royal robes closer about himself and replied, "He has left to see if he can get ships from the King of France for his foolish voyage. Imagine anyone thinking he can find a short way to the Far East by sailing west across the ocean.

9

"For the past six years he has been here in Spain trying to get ships, men, and supplies for his expedition. King John of Portugal did not believe his plan would succeed and refused to give him aid. Our own committee has listened patiently to all his grand ideas, but our advisors are certain that his plan is ridiculous. When his ships sail out to sea, they will disappear over the edge of the world and we shall never hear from them again. Let the King of France throw away his money if he wants to do it. Columbus will have no ships from me."

"But, Sire, I am sure that the world is round," replied the queen. "Those who say it is flat do not know. I have just received a letter from my old confessor Juan Perez about Columbus. I now believe that Columbus can reach the riches of the Far East by sailing west. Would you let the King of France gain those riches that we here in Spain need so much? Besides, our priests will go with Columbus to carry the word of God to those heathen. We must send for Columbus at once. He shall sail this very year under the flag of Castile and Aragon."

Thus, if it had not been for Isabella and her belief that the world was round and that Columbus could reach the Far East by sailing west, the whole course of history would have been changed.

Isabella was born 500 years ago. She was the daughter of King John of Castile. In those days Spain was not a united nation. Castile was like a separate and independent state in Spain. Much of Spain was in the hands of the Moors, who had invaded the country from Africa and for hundreds of years had occupied the land. They were Mohammedans.

When the King of Castile died in 1474, his beautiful, 23-year-old daughter, Isabella, became Queen of Castile and Leon. At the age of eighteen she had married the handsome Ferdinand of Aragon, thus uniting two of the most powerful royal families in Spain. She was an ardent Catholic and did everything possible to extend that faith throughout her kingdom.

When Columbus was refused aid by the King of Portugal, he came to Spain in 1485. At that time Castile and Leon were at war with the Moors in a desperate attempt to drive them out of Spain. Queen Isabella and King Ferdinand were so busy that they had no time to listen to any plans to outfit a voyage into unknown seas.

Columbus, however, was not easily discouraged. Year after year he followed the court from place to place, pleading for money to outfit the ships for his voyage of discovery. He was told that he would have to wait until the Moors had been conquered before he would get the money.

At the end of six years, Columbus thought that there was no use waiting any longer, and he decided to go to see the King of France. On the way he stopped at the monastery of La Rabida. There Juan Perez, who had once been the queen's confessor, begged Columbus not to go on to France until he had written to the queen urging her to listen to Columbus' plans.

Queen Isabella read the letter and sent for Columbus. He arrived at Granada, where the queen was staying, in time to see the Moors surrender. Now that the war was over and Isabella was Queen of Spain, she was willing to help Columbus for the greater glory of her beloved land and to spread the Catholic faith.

"But, your Majesty, this will cost much money," said her advisors. "The war with the Moors has taken most of our gold so that there is little left for such a foolish trip."

13

"Columbus will succeed," replied Queen Isabella. "He will bring us fame and fortune. If there are no more funds in the Treasury, take these jewels of mine. Go now, they will bring more than enough money for this brave admiral's needs."

You have already read in your books how Columbus sailed from Spain in August of that year, 1492. Although he never reached the Far East, he did discover America on October 12. The Spanish explorers who followed Columbus to the New World brought back riches far greater than any Isabella had even dreamed of. Also the Catholic faith was extended by Isabella, not only throughout Spain, but throughout Central and South America as well.

Queen Isabella was one of Spain's most brilliant queens and laid the foundation for Spain's greatest period of glory. Her faith in Columbus and her willingness to

"Take these jewels for this brave admiral's needs."

part with her jewels so that he could make his famous voyage led to the discovery of America.

QUEEN ELIZABETH

No book of famous women would be complete without a story about "Good Queen Bess" who made it possible for the English to establish their colonies in America. Although she became Queen of England at the age of 26 and ruled for 45 years, her reign and even her life were often in danger.

Elizabeth was born in 1533, the daughter of King Henry the Eighth and Anne Boleyn. After the death of King Henry in 1547, the throne of England was occupied by Edward and then Mary. In 1558, Queen Mary died without leaving any children

17

and Elizabeth was crowned Queen. At that time the fortunes of England were at a low point caused by troubles over religious matters and conflicts with Scotland and Ireland. Across the channel there was fighting in France and The Netherlands.

Elizabeth was a brilliant young woman when she became Queen, and her reign was one of the most glorious in the history of England. It was during this period that the arts and literature were encouraged throughout England, housing was greatly improved, and England laid the foundation for the vast colonial empire which it later built up overseas.

Spain had already established its colonies in Mexico and South America. The wealth of Latin America was being brought back in Spanish ships to enrich the royal treasury. English sea captains wanted that gold and silver and planned to capture some of the Spanish ships.

At that time England was not at war with Spain, so Elizabeth had to shut her eyes to the deeds of her daring sea captains like Hawkins, Drake, Frobisher, and Raleigh. They sailed out privately from English ports and captured as many Spanish treasure ships as they could. English ships could be found in almost every part of the world.

Since Elizabeth never married, she was called the "Virgin Queen." When Sir Walter Raleigh set out in 1585 to found a colony in America, he called it *Virginia* in honor of the Virgin Queen. It was Raleigh who brought back the potato and tobacco from the New World and introduced them into England.

One of the most daring of the Elizabethan sea captains was Francis Drake. He sailed on several expeditions to the West Indies and the Spanish settlements on the shores of the Caribbean Sea. He was able to capture several Spanish vessels laden with treasure which he brought back to England.

In 1577, he sailed with five ships to attack the Spanish in the Pacific. He rounded Cape Horn and sailed up the west coast of South America, attacking the Spanish settlements and capturing Spanish vessels wherever he could. Sailing up the North American Coast as far as Puget Sound, he laid claim to the Pacific Northwest Territory in the name of Queen Elizabeth.

Turning his ship westward, Drake sailed across the Pacific and Indian Oceans, rounded the Cape of Good Hope, and returned to England at last after having been gone for three years. He was the first Englishman to sail around the world.

Queen Elizabeth was so delighted with Drake's daring adventures which added so much to the growing fame of England on the seas that she visited his ship and

Queen Elizabeth made Francis Drake a knight.

dined aboard. After dinner she surprised him by making him a knight. After that he was known as Sir Francis Drake. As a Vice Admiral in Her Majesty's Navy, he continued to win fame in his naval victories over the Spanish.

Queen Elizabeth's reign was noted as a period in which English literature reached new heights. It has been called the "Golden Age" in English literature. Those were the days of Edmund Spenser, Sir Francis Bacon, and William Shakespeare. The great tragedies and comedies written by Shakespeare, and in which he himself acted, are still read in almost every school as an example of the best in English literature. Queen Elizabeth often commanded Shakespeare to perform his plays for her. She enjoyed them just as much as we do today.

Elizabeth never married, but many princes hoped that they could win her hand. She kept them all guessing. One day she would hint that she would marry—the next day she would change her mind. The people of England hoped that she would marry. Even the British Parliament suggested that it would be a good thing if she should wed and have a son and heir to the throne.

But in those stormy times, Elizabeth thought that it would be better if she could keep peace with the other countries of Europe by holding out to their ruling princes the hope that she would marry one of them. Philip of Spain was one who hoped he might be successful. King Henry VIII of England had married a Spanish princess, the granddaughter of Queen Isabella and King Ferdinand of Aragon. Why shouldn't Elizabeth marry a Spanish King?

Even though England's sea captains, like Hawkins and Drake, were plundering his Spanish treasure ships, Philip dared not declare war on England so long as there was a chance of marrying Elizabeth. At that time Spain was one of the greatest naval forces in the world, while England had yet to prove herself "Mistress of the Seas." Philip fretted with anger, but he waited year after year, hoping to win the hand of Elizabeth.

Finally, in 1588, Philip could stand it no longer. He decided to put a stop to the English piracy in Latin America and to prevent the British from sending aid to the people of The Netherlands who had revolted against Spain, which then controlled that country. He assembled one of the greatest fleets of fighting ships that the world had ever seen. This huge armada was made up of 120 large, clumsy sailing ships that carried many soldiers for close fighting but were difficult to maneuver.

Queen Elizabeth sent word to her admirals, Drake, Hawkins, and Frobisher, that this Spanish fleet must be destroyed. The English fleet was small, but the ships were of the newer type that had been built to sail fast, maneuver quickly, and carry heavy guns. Besides, the English sea captains were the best in the world and were determined to save England at all costs.

The slow-sailing Spanish fleet was no match for the fast British ships which sailed out to meet them. To add to the destruction, a mighty storm arose which helped to wreck the Spanish Armada. Only 54 of the original 120 ships of the Spanish fleet were able to escape and return to Spain. It was one of the greatest sea battles in history.

Spain's once mighty seapower was crippled forever. It was no longer a threat to the British. Queen Elizabeth's fleet thus laid the foundation for Britain's mighty navy that was to rule the seas for many years and made it possible for England to establish her colonies in America and throughout the world.

WHAT DO YOU THINK?

1. Why is Joan of Arc often called the "Maid of Orleans?"

2. Why is the story of Joan of Arc inspiring?

3. How do you think Joan of Arc was able to defeat the English?

4. What finally happened to Joan of Arc?

5. In Columbus' time what did most people think about the shape of the earth?

6. What did Columbus think about the shape of the earth?

7. Why did Columbus think that he could reach the Far East by sailing west from Europe?

8. What were two of the reasons why Queen Isabella helped Columbus?

9. When was America discovered? By whom?

10. Why is Queen Elizabeth's reign considered one of the most glorious periods in the history of England?

11. Why is the Elizabethan period called the "Golden Age" in English literature?

12. How did Queen Elizabeth's fleet make possible the founding of English colonies in America?

13. Who do you think had the greatest influence upon the history of the world—Joan, Isabella, or Elizabeth? Why?

WHAT DO THESE WORDS MEAN?

Tell what each of these words means. Use each word in a sentence. If you are not sure of the meaning or the pronunciation of a word, look it up in a dictionary.

1. armada	5. divine	9. monastery
2. ardent	6. enrich	10. Majesty
3. advisors	7. heathen	11. Sire
4. clad	8. Mohammedan	12. reign

WHY WERE THESE EVENTS IMPORTANT?

If you are not sure of these events, look them up in an encyclopedia.

1. Battle of Agincourt
2. Surrender of the Moors in Spain
3. Battle of Orleans
4. Columbus' discovery of America
5. Destruction of Spanish Armada
6. Drake"s voyage around the world

POCAHONTAS

When the first English settlers arrived in Jamestown, Virginia, in 1607, they found the woods filled with Indians ruled by a powerful chief, named Powhatan. The Indians did not like to have the white men shoot the deer in the forests. Often the Indians could not find anything left to shoot with their bows and arrows and so were without food. They hated the white men who had taken their land.

But there was one Indian who did not hate the white men. This was Pocahontas —the young and beautiful princess— daughter of Powhatan. Her real name was

Matoaka, but she was called Pocahontas, which means "tomboy" in the Indian language, because she was as brave and daring as any of the young warriors.

She listened to the stories that the Indians told of these strangers who had come to their shore in a great canoe—far bigger than the chief's canoe. The white men's boat had great white sails like the wings of a bird that carried the big canoe along with the wind. These white men wore strange clothes and could kill a deer with magic just by pointing at it with something that looked like a stick. Pocahontas was amazed at these wonderful tales and looked forward to the time when she would see these things herself.

One day the Indians captured the leader of the English colony, Captain John Smith. He had nearly escaped by seizing one of the Indians and holding him so that he served as protection. Smith then began to fight his way back toward his boat. All would have gone well if Smith had not fallen into a swamp where he was taken prisoner by the Indians and brought back to their chief, Powhatan.

Dressed in furs and wearing his royal crown of red feathers, Powhatan called a council together to decide what to do with the prisoner. All the Indians of the tribe gathered around to hear how the great white chief had been captured after a fight in which one of the Indians had been killed.

"One of our brothers has been killed," said Powhatan, "so this man must die."

"Kill, kill, kill," shouted all the Indian warriors who were seated around the council fire.

John Smith realized that there was little hope of his being rescued. His hands and his feet were tied together, and his head was forced down upon a stone which was used by the Indians when they clubbed prisoners to death. Above him stood a powerful Indian with a war club upraised in his hands.

"This is the end," thought Smith.

But just then Pocahontas dashed forward and threw herself on the prisoner.

"Spare the life of this great white chief!" begged the Indian princess. "He is a brave man. Let us adopt him into our tribe."

Powhatan loved his daughter dearly. If she wanted to save this man's life, he would grant her request. Captain John Smith was set free and later returned to Jamestown. Under his able leadership, the little settlement succeeded. It became the important colony of Virginia.

Pocahontas was very helpful to the growing settlement. She brought food when the people were in danger of starving. She warned the English when the Indians planned to attack. She visited James-

"Spare the life of this great white chief!"

town often. The English settlers were glad to have this beautiful Indian princess come to see them. One of the settlers, John Rolfe, fell in love with her.

Captain John Smith had been wounded and had returned to England for medical treatment. Besides, he was growing old and probably would not return to Jamestown. With Smith out of the way, John Rolfe was sure he could win the beautiful Indian princess. One night as they sat in the moonlight, he whispered in her ear, "Pocahontas, I love you. Will you marry me?"

"Yes," she replied, for she had come to love the handsome young Englishman.

Powhatan was angry at first that she had not chosen one of his Indian braves for her husband, but he finally consented to the marriage.

All the English settlers and many of the Indians came to the wedding in the little

34

church at Jamestown whose crumbling walls are still standing there. Everyone knew that this wedding would bring peace and trade between the English and the Indians.

John Rolfe and his lovely wife moved out to a plantation on the James River where he raised tobacco—the first tobacco to be grown by any of the colonists. This could be sold at a good price in England. Soon other colonists started growing tobacco and Virginia prospered. It is still one of the great tobacco producing states in the Union.

A few years later, John Rolfe and Pocahontas and their little son, Thomas, sailed for England. There the Indian princess was entertained by the King and Queen, but Pocahontas longed for the forests and plantations of Virginia. She was taken sick and died in England before she could return to her native America that she loved so well. She was buried in England, but her son returned to America. Today some of Virginia's finest citizens are proud to claim Pocahontas as their ancestor.

HOW THE CAPTAIN
LOST A WIFE

PRISCILLA

You have read how Captain John Smith and a group of Englishmen founded the first English colony in America at Jamestown, Virginia, in 1607. These colonists came in search of gold, but found none. You have also read how their leader was saved from death by the beautiful Indian Princess, Pocahontas. Perhaps if John Smith had been younger or had not been wounded so that he was forced to return to England, the two would have been married. Instead, Pocahontas married the handsome young John Rolfe.

A few years later, in 1620, another group of Englishmen came to America. They landed at Plymouth Rock near Cape Cod and founded a settlement that was later to grow into the Massachusetts Colony. These people were not looking for gold. They had come to America to find a new home where they could worship God as they pleased. The military leader of this settlement was Captain Miles Standish. The poet, Henry Longfellow, in his lovely poem, *The Courtship of Miles Standish,* tells one of the most charming of love stories and has made Priscilla famous.

The Pilgrims who founded the Plymouth Colony were English men and women who wished to worship God in their own way. They did not want to go to the Church of England under the control of the king. This angered King James and he threatened to arrest them, so they fled to Holland.

The Pilgrims stayed there for some years. But when their children began to grow up speaking Dutch and adopting Dutch customs, the Pilgrims decided to leave the country and find a new home in America, where they could have English ways and yet worship as they pleased.

In 1620 they sailed for America in the *Mayflower*. It was winter before they reached Cape Cod in Massachusetts. They had intended to go farther south, but because of the bad weather, they decided to land there. The Pilgrims had a very hard time during that first terrible winter, and many, including Rose Standish, the Captain's wife, died of cold, hunger, and sickness.

When spring came, the Pilgrims cleared the land and planted their crops. The warm sun cheered the colonists and made the crops grow. That fall the settlers were delighted with their fine harvest and decided to have a feast and give thanks to God for His many blessings. It was the first Thanksgiving Day, a holiday which we still celebrate each November.

There had been no serious attacks by the Indians. Captain Miles Standish was becoming weary and lonely. He thought that perhaps it would be a good thing if he married again, so he began looking over the pretty girls of Plymouth. Among these, the loveliest was Priscilla Mullens. Miles Standish saw her sitting in her doorway spinning the wool of the sheep into thread which would later be dyed and woven into cloth. On Sundays he would see her going to the church on the hill. "What a wonderful wife she would be," thought Miles Standish.

The captain was then about forty years old. He was an excellent soldier, but he did not know what to say to pretty young girls. Would Priscilla listen to him? He was not sure, but then he had a good idea. Why not send John Alden? John was a handsome young man who lived at his house. Surely Priscilla would listen to him.

So he spoke to John Alden one day. "John, since Rose died, my life has been weary and dreary. Often have I thought of Priscilla. She is alone in the world. Her father and mother died during that first terrible winter. I would like to make Priscilla my wife. But I am a soldier; I wouldn't know just how to ask her. You have read in your books how to propose to a girl. Go, tell her that Captain Miles Standish, a man of action, not words, offers her his hand and his heart in marriage."

Now John was shy. He loved Priscilla with all his heart but was too bashful to tell her so. For some time he himself had been waiting for a chance to ask Priscilla to be his wife, so he was greatly upset when the old Captain asked him to speak to her. "Oh, I can't do that. You would do much better if you asked her yourself," replied John.

"Nonsense," said the Captain. "You know just what to say. You who have been my friend for so long cannot refuse to do this for me."

"Well, I will ask her if you insist," said John.

"What shall I do?" said John to himself as he set out for the cottage where Priscilla lived. "I love her dearly, and yet in the name of friendship I shall have to tell Priscilla that Captain Miles Standish wants to marry her. She is all alone in the world and will probably accept the Captain's offer. Oh, what shall I do? I love her and cannot live without her."

Priscilla welcomed the shy but handsome John Alden thinking that perhaps at last he had come to ask her to marry him.

There was a ship leaving for England the next morning and for a while they talked about that. "I have been thinking of going back to England," said Priscilla, trying to give the young man a hint of how she felt. "I am so lonely here all alone."

"I don't blame you for being lonely," said John, "and I have come to ask your hand in marriage."

Priscilla's heart beat faster. This was the moment for which she had been waiting. At last her dreams had come true. Now she would be Mrs. Alden, but all she could say was, "Oh, John!"

"Yes," continued John Alden as calmly as he could. "I have come to ask for your hand in marriage for my good friend, Captain Miles Standish."

Priscilla was disappointed. She would not marry a man twice her age. "If the great Captain of Plymouth is so very eager to wed me, why does he not come himself?" said Priscilla with a smile, trying to hide her disappointment.

John Alden tried to explain that the Captain would have come if he weren't so busy, but that only made matters worse.

"Why don't you speak for yourself, John?" asked Priscilla.

John could not do that because he had promised Miles Standish that he would speak for him, so instead of replying, the bashful man grabbed his hat and fled down the path away from the cottage.

Captain Miles Standish was furious when he heard what had happened. Things would have gone badly for John if at that moment the Captain had not been called away to attend an important meeting.

An Indian messenger had just arrived in Plymouth bringing a rattlesnake's skin filled with arrows. This was a sign from a near-by Indian Chief that he would declare war unless the Pilgrims were willing

44

"Why don't you speak for yourself, John?"

to accept his terms. The Pilgrims had just about decided to surrender to the Chief's terms when Miles Standish entered and shouted, "No! Let me take charge of this matter. If the Indians want to fight, we will fight."

Seizing the rattlesnake's skin, he emptied out the arrows and filled it with powder and shot. Then he handed it back to the messenger to take back to his chief.

Not waiting for further word from the Indians, Captain Miles Standish set out to attack them first. He was gone for many days on this successful expedition which prevented an Indian war. But before he returned, a false report was received in Plymouth that he had been shot by the Indians with a poisoned arrow and had died.

Although John Alden grieved for his friend, he was now free to ask Priscilla to be his wife. He went over to her cottage where Priscilla was sitting at her spinning wheel. John Alden asked, "Have you heard the news? Captain Miles Standish is dead. Now, I can speak for myself. Will you marry me, Priscilla?"

The two immediately arranged for the wedding. As the happy couple left the church as man and wife, they saw Captain Miles Standish returning from his expedition. What did the Captain do? If you read the poem, "The Courtship of Miles Standish," you will find out.

ANNE HUTCHINSON

The Pilgrims, who founded the Plymouth Colony in 1620, and the Puritans,
who settled the Massachusetts Bay Colony
a few years later, came to America to find
a new home where they could worship
God as they thought best. They did not
think the King of England was right in
trying to force them to attend the Church
of England. But, when the Puritans had
established their colony in Massachusetts,
they were not tolerant of those who differed
from them in religious matters.

The Puritans were a God-fearing,
stern, and strict group of men and women

who laid the foundation for a prosperous New England in America. They wanted only those people in their colony who believed as they did.

It was in Salem, Massachusetts, that a group of children one day declared that an old woman was a witch and had tried to cast an evil spell on them. Today we can laugh at such foolish and childish ideas, but in Massachusetts in those days many people believed that there really were witches who could talk with the devil. The Puritans didn't want any witches in their colony. Before the people realized that they were wrong in accusing these women of being witches, many old women had been ducked into the water to clean their souls, and others had been put to death.

The religious leaders of Massachusetts were sure that they were doing right when they drove people out of the colony who did not believe as they did. In 1635 a young minister in Salem, named Roger Williams, offended the Puritan leaders by preaching that there should be religious freedom and that a person should be able to worship as he believed was right. The Puritans planned to send him back to England, but Roger Williams fled from Massachusetts on a cold wintry day in 1636 and took refuge with an Indian tribe on Narragansett Bay.

There he founded a settlement which he called *Providence* to show his thanks to God for protecting him. Soon the colony grew, and the name was changed to Rhode Island and the Providence Plantations. Everyone who wanted to come to the colony was welcome. It made no difference to what church he belonged. He could live peaceably in Rhode Island.

About this time there lived near Boston, Massachusetts, a young woman, named Mrs. Anne Hutchinson, who believed in religious freedom. Before she was married, her name was Anne Marbury. She was born in England near the town of Boston in that country. Her father was a Puritan minister who had preached there and in London.

As a little girl she used to go to church on Sundays and listen to her father preach. Often during the week her mother and father would discuss the sermons. Anne would sit nearby and listen. Then she would play with her dolls pretending that she was a preacher and that they had come to church to listen to her.

At an early age she married William Hutchinson. Then when so many of the Puritans began leaving England to go to America so they would have a place where they could worship as they pleased, the Hutchinsons packed up all their things and made plans to go, too. In 1634 they left old Boston, England, with their children and all their household goods and sailed for Boston, Massachusetts. After a stormy voyage of seven weeks, they at last arrived safely.

Mrs. Hutchinson took an active part in the social life of Boston. Soon she began to organize meetings for women at which they would talk over the sermons that had been preached the previous Sunday. Anne Hutchinson did not always agree with what the preacher had said, and she was not afraid to tell the ladies at her meetings what she thought.

In those days the Puritans were in control in Massachusetts, and Puritan preachers did not like to have anyone criticize what they said or did. Some of the colonists agreed with their Puritan ministers. Others agreed with Anne Hutchinson. The colony was in danger of being divided, so the ministers and judges met at Cambridge just outside of Boston.

For three weeks they discussed what they should do about Anne Hutchinson. Finally they decided that she could no longer hold her meetings for women. They said that she must not speak in public.

Anne Hutchinson continued to hold meetings at her house, so in October, 1637, she was brought to trial before the General Court of Massachusetts and sentenced to be banished from the colony. In March, 1638, she fled from Massachusetts to Rhode Island with her husband and family and seventy friends. Roger Williams welcomed them. They bought an island from the Indians and lived there until the death of William Hutchinson four years later.

Hearing that Massachusetts was trying to get control of Rhode Island, Anne Hutchinson decided to move to the Dutch settlement in what is now New York.

She lived in a log cabin on the outskirts

of New Amsterdam. The Dutch left her alone on her little farm. Everything seemed peaceful, and she was happy with her family and small group of friends.

One day an Indian war whoop was heard ringing through the woods. What could it mean? The Indians had not troubled her before. They had always seemed friendly enough, but this was different. The Dutch were miles away. There was no one to call for help.

Anne Hutchinson gathered her children about her and ran into her cabin, bolting the door behind her. Peering through the windows, she could see a band of Indians with their faces smeared with red war paint. They were swinging their heavy clubs and yelling their war cries. Anne was frightened. What could she do? Where could she turn for help? The Indians were now at her door. With their war clubs they smashed it down, rushed in,

The Indians were now at her door.

and dragged the women out. Anne and her whole family of fifteen persons were taken prisoners, and all but one daughter were put to death.

Today the river that ran near her little cabin is called the Hutchinson River in her honor, and a modern new parkway that extends from New York City up through Connecticut is named the Hutchinson River Parkway. How many of the millions of motorists that drive on this fine new road today think of the courageous woman who once lived nearby in what was then wilderness, so that she could have religious freedom and worship God as she thought best?

NOW TRY THESE?

1. How did Pocahontas save the life of Captain John Smith?

2. How did Pocahontas help the first English colony in America?

3. If you had been John Alden, what would you have done when the Captain asked you to speak to Priscilla for him?

4. Why did Priscilla say, "Why don't you speak for yourself, John?"

5. If you were Priscilla, whom would you have married? Why?

6. What is a spinning wheel? How is it used?

7. Tell how the Indian Chief threatened war and what happened.

8. If you had been the captain, what would you have done upon returning to Plymouth?

9. Tell how the early settlers in Salem treated those whom they thought were witches.

10. What did the religious leaders in the Massachusetts Bay Colony do to people who did not believe as they did?

11. Why did Roger Williams found Rhode Island?

12. What happened to Anne Hutchinson?

USE THESE WORDS IN SENTENCES

1. amazed	8. discuss	16. social life
2. banished	9. able leadership	17. organize
3. bashful	10. called a council	18. prosper-
4. calmly	11. hand in marriage	ous
5. courageous	12. medical treatment	19. sermons
6. courtship	13. religious freedom	20. tolerant
7. criticize	14. religious leaders	21. worship
	15. greatly upset	

MATCHING GAME

Here is a list of some early American colonies: Jamestown, Virginia, Plymouth, Massachusetts Bay, Rhode Island, New Amsterdam (New York).

Now match each of the following with the colony with which they were closely associated.
Example: Priscilla-Plymouth.

1. Pocahontas	7. Boston
2. John Smith	8. First tobacco
3. *Mayflower*	9. Roger Williams
4. witches	10. Anne Hutchinson
5. Pilgrims	11. Narragansett Bay
6. Puritans	12. First Thanksgiving

THE FIRST
STARS AND STRIPES

BETSY ROSS

Whenever you see the Stars and Stripes waving proudly in the breeze, you should think of Betsy Ross, who made the first American flag in 1777.

Betsy was the eighth child born in the Quaker family of Griscom. The Griscoms had a large family of sixteen children, so there was plenty of work to be done around the house. Betsy helped her mother with the mending and sewing until she married and moved to a home of her own at 229 Arch Street. It was in that small, old-fashioned brick house that she lived with her husband, John Ross, during the Revolutionary War. He had a small upholstery store, while Betsy sewed and made flags.

On July 4, 1776, the Continental Congress met in Philadelphia and adopted the Declaration of Independence which declared, "These United Colonies are, and of right ought to be, free and independent states." Now that the United States of America was a free nation, it was felt that there should be an American flag. On June 14, 1777, the Congress adopted a flag and agreed that it was to have "thirteen stripes, alternate white and red, and that the Union be thirteen white stars on a blue field."

A committee was appointed to arrange to have the first flag made. The committee, headed by George Washington, included Robert Morris and General George Ross, an uncle of John Ross. These men visited

Mrs. Ross, and, seated around the old open fireplace in the corner, they planned the new flag.

The first thing to be decided upon was the shape of the stars. George Washington suggested a six-pointed star because it would be easy to cut out of cloth.

"But a five-pointed star is much prettier," said Betsy Ross, "and it is just as easy to cut. Here, let me show you." She took a piece of white cloth and folded it. Then, with one snip of her scissors, she held out a perfect five-pointed star. George Washington was delighted, and the committee quickly agreed to use the five-pointed star.

Congress had said that the new flag should have thirteen stripes, alternate white and red, so Betsy Ross started with a white stripe and added a red stripe and then another white stripe until she had thirteen stripes. This meant that there was a white stripe at both the top and the bottom of the flag. "Would it not be better if there was a red stripe at the top and bottom?" said George Washington. "The flag would stay clean longer and the edges would be more easily seen when the flag was flying."

Everybody agreed, so Betsy started again with a red stripe at the top. This meant that the flag would have seven red stripes and six white stripes. Then they tried stripes of different sizes. The flag that looked best was one with each stripe six inches wide. This meant that the flag with 13 stripes was 6 feet, 6 inches in height. They decided that the length of the flag should be half again as long.

Betsy Ross made the blue field in the upper left-hand corner the height of seven stripes, or $3\frac{1}{2}$ feet high and just a little longer than it was high. Now the only thing that remained was how to arrange the stars. They tried placing the stars in

Betsy Ross made the first American flag.

different ways and finally agreed upon arranging them in a circle.

Betsy Ross had made the first flag so well that the government gave her a contract to make all of its flags. She continued making American flags until her death in 1836.

On the 4th of July, 1777, John Paul Jones was placed in charge of the United States Warship *Ranger*. When he was ready to sail, the ship had no flag, so the girls of the town decided that he must have a flag like the one Betsy Ross had just made. They cut up their best dresses of red, white, and blue and sewed together the pieces of silk. When the flag was finished, they gave it to Captain Jones. It was the first Stars and Stripes ever raised on a United States man-of-war. With his new ship proudly flying the new flag, John Paul Jones sailed for England to attack the British in their home waters. In many daring adventures and successful sea battles, John Paul Jones brought great honor and glory to the United States Navy and the flag that he flew.

The thirteen stars and the thirteen stripes represented the original thirteen states. In those days the people had no idea that someday the United States would stretch from the Atlantic to the Pacific and include 48 states. At that time the thirteen states were all located along the Atlantic Coast, and few people lived west of the Allegheny Mountains. When the pioneers started moving inland and Kentucky and Vermont entered the Union, two more stripes and two more stars were added to the flag.

Later, as new states asked to join the Union, Congress realized that it would be unwise to keep on adding stars and stripes to the flag. In 1818 Congress passed a law that the flag of the United States should forever after have thirteen stripes like the one that Betsy Ross had first made but that a new star should be added for each new state.

THE FIGHT
FOR INDEPENDENCE

MOLLY PITCHER

During the Revolutionary War while the little American army was fighting so valiantly for independence from England, the daughters, wives, sweethearts, and mothers of the soldiers helped at home. They made clothes for the soldiers, took charge of the farms, cared for the sick and wounded, and raised money to help win the war. But there was at least one woman who did more. She became famous by actually going into battle and helping fire the guns.

If you ever visit the battlefield at Monmouth, New Jersey, where an important battle of the Revolutionary War was fought, you will find a monument to this famous woman of the War of Independence—Molly Pitcher.

Molly was born in Carlisle, Pennsylvania, about 1744. Her real name was Mary Ludwig. When the Revolutionary War broke out, she was happily married and living on a farm with her husband, John Hays. When John left to help George Washington in America's fight for freedom, Molly went along, too.

Molly Hays helped to take care of the camp and assisted with the cooking. During a battle, she brought food and water to the men who worked with her husband in the artillery.

If the day was hot and the men could not leave their guns to find water for a cooling drink, Molly would run to a near-

Soon everybody was calling to her, "Molly, pitcher!"

by spring or well and come back with a pitcher of cool water. The weary, thirsty soldiers were always glad to see Molly coming down the road with her pitcher. You could hear them shout, "Here comes Molly with her pitcher!" "Molly, bring the pitcher over here!" Soon everybody was calling to her, "Molly, pitcher!" It was not long before she was known throughout the regiment as Molly Pitcher.

Molly Pitcher's husband was in charge of a cannon. At the Battle of Monmouth he fell wounded as the British charged forward to capture the gun and put it out of action. When Molly saw her husband fall to the ground, she rushed to save the cannon and continued firing it. The enemy was driven back and the cannon was safe.

George Washington, who was directing the battle from horseback nearby, saw the brave Molly Pitcher take her husband's place. After the battle he sent for her.

"If all my soldiers are as brave as you, Molly Pitcher," said George Washington, "we shall soon drive the British from our fair land. For your gallant deeds today, I hereby promote you to the rank of sergeant."

Molly was very proud to be promoted by General George Washington himself and remained with the army for several years. She had many other exciting adventures.

After the War for Independence was won, she returned to Carlisle. She died there in 1823.

MARY LINDLEY MURRAY

While there were some women like Molly Pitcher and Margaret Corbin who took part in the actual fighting during the Revolutionary War, there were many others who helped just as much to win the war while staying home. Such a person was Mary Lindley Murray.

Mary Lindley was a beautiful Quaker maid who grew up in Philadelphia. She married a wealthy businessman, named Robert Murray. In 1753 they moved to New York while it was still an English colony. Mr. Murray formed a company with Mr. Sansom, and the firm of Murray and Sansom became one of the best known in New York City.

Mrs. Murray went to England and lived there for some years but returned to New York during the first year of the War of Independence. Although the wealthy Mr. Murray favored the British, his wife was anxious to help George Washington and the colonies win their freedom from England.

The Murrays had a beautiful home not far south of where the Grand Central Station now stands on 42nd Street. This section is still known as Murray Hill. Today the crowded streets and tall buildings there shut out any distant view. In 1776, however, the Murrays could look from their windows across Manhattan Island to the East River.

In August of that year the British troops had landed on Long Island. A battle was fought there where the Borough of Brooklyn stands today. The little American army was badly defeated and had to retreat. The British waited for the dawn of another day to attack again. They were sure that the next morning they could force Washington to surrender and end the war, for there seemed no way for the Americans to escape.

But during the night, under cover of a heavy fog, the entire American army was rowed across the East River to the Manhattan side. When the British awoke, the fog was beginning to clear away. They could see the last boatload of American soldiers nearing the opposite bank of the river. The American army had escaped.

The British did not follow immediately. The Americans had lost the battle, and the British were sure that they could cross the river and capture what was left of the American army whenever they wished.

On September 15th Mrs. Murray looked out of her window and saw the British soldiers starting out in their boats to cross the river to Manhattan. There were so many that she knew the little American army would be no match for them. Five big British warships had sailed up the East River to silence the American guns on shore and to provide protection for the English soldiers as they landed. The Americans had to retreat again.

The main body of the Americans, under George Washington, was encamped several miles to the north. They were so few, however, that they could not spare any men to try to withstand the main attack of the British.

On the southern tip of Manhattan Island was General Putnam with the rest of the American forces. If the British marched across Manhattan and separated Putnam's divisions from those of Washington's, Putnam would be forced to surrender with his 4,000 men. This would so cripple the American army that Washington might then have to surrender too.

General Washington realized the danger to Putnam's troops and hurriedly sent word for him to retreat northward immediately to join the main body of troops and avoid the British attack.

Mrs. Murray, too, realized that the British were preparing a trap to catch Putnam's men. What could she do to prevent it? Oh, if she could only think of something! Then she had an idea.

She quickly sent one of her servants to the top of the house to keep her informed of Putnam's progress. The dust kicked up by Putnam's men as they marched northward up Broadway on the west side of Manhattan could be seen from the upper windows of the Murray mansion.

Then, putting on her prettiest gown, she

sent word to the British General Howe that she would be deeply honored if the brave general and his officers would stop for a moment at her home while she served them some cool drinks.

General Howe had met the beautiful and witty Mrs. Murray when she was in England. He would indeed have liked to stop, for the day was hot for that time of year. He rode up to the Murray mansion and saw Mrs. Murray smiling down at him from the porch.

"I wish I could accept your kind invitation," said the gallant general, "but I must be on my way to capture Putnam and his Yankees."

"It is too bad that you did not come sooner," replied Mrs. Murray. "Haven't you heard that he has already marched northward to join Washington? Stay and dine with me. There will be time enough to catch Putnam later."

"If that is the case," replied Howe, "my officers and I shall be delighted to join you."

Mrs. Murray smiled her sweetest at the officers that day. She listened to their stories of how they had driven back the Americans. She laughed at all their jokes. She served them the best food in the house and the choicest wines, so that the British forgot about Putnam and his men.

At last, when the servant sent word for her to come to the tower in the house, she excused herself and ran up the stairs to the top floor. Sure enough, the American troops of Putnam were now far to the north and safely on their way to join Washington. Mrs. Murray had saved the American army of four thousand men to fight again.

Although Washington's troops had been discouraged after their defeat on Long Island, they now took heart when they saw Putnam at the head of his men come

"I shall be delighted to join you."

marching into camp. Many battles were still to be fought, but the Americans, cheered by Mrs. Murray's clever trick, fought on and finally won their independence from England.

BETTY ZANE

Another famous woman of the American Revolution was Betty Zane. Her brave deeds will never be forgotten. Her father, Colonel Zane, who later helped to lay out the city of Zanesville, Ohio, built Fort Henry in 1769. This was the first American settlement on the Ohio River, which became such an important waterway for the early pioneers as they moved west into Kentucky, southern Indiana, Illinois, and the Mississippi Valley. The City of Wheeling, West Virginia, now stands on the site of old Fort Henry.

During the Revolutionary War, the British stirred up the Indians and encouraged them to attack the frontier settlements of the Americans. One day a messenger appeared at Fort Henry to report that the Indians were again on the warpath.

The settlers fled to the fort for safety and barred and bolted the huge wooden gate to the stockade. Colonel Zane gave orders that the women and children should keep out of sight while the men made ready to take their places in the blockhouse and around the stockade. It was not long before 500 savages in war paint appeared out of the woods in front of Fort Henry. They were led by Simon Girty, who had lived with the Indians for many years. Although the men of the fort were greatly outnumbered, they felt they could withstand the attack of the Indians until help arrived.

The Indians did not wait long. With a wild yell they rushed forward, shooting their arrows as they closed in on the fort. Colonel Zane and his men withheld their fire until the savages were almost upon them. Then, at a signal, the defenders opened fire at short range. Each shot sped to its mark, and the Indians retreated to the woods to reassemble their forces.

The Indians attacked again and again. Each time the men in the fort were able to drive them off. But now the supply of powder in the fort was running low. The settlers could not hold out much longer. Outside the Indians were yelling with rage because so many of their warriors had been killed. If they captured the fort, they would be sure to torture and kill every one of the settlers. What could the defenders of the fort do now that they had no powder for their guns?

Then one of the men remembered that there was a small keg of powder in his log cabin outside the fort. Someone must try to get it, but who would dare to go and run the chance of almost certain death from the savages outside? Colonel Zane asked for volunteers.

When his young daughter, Betty Zane, heard that someone was needed to get the powder, she ran to her father and said, "Let me go! Not a man can be spared! Let me go! I am not afraid."

Her father knew that it meant sure death if she were captured by the Indians and hesitated to let her go.

"But, Father, you need every man here to fight the Indians. It is better that I go," begged Betty.

"Maybe you are right," replied her father sadly. "You may go. We will do everything we can to cover you with our guns to prevent the savages from capturing you. Maybe you can get through. May God be with you."

The bars were taken from the gates, and

The settlers depended on her to get that powder back.

Betty slipped through. She ran as fast as she could to the log cabin where the powder was hidden. She hoped that the Indians would not see her. Not a sound was heard until she started back with the precious keg of powder in her arms.

Suddenly an Indian cry was heard, and the arrows began whizzing around her head. Then a group of savages came running toward her from the woods.

Betty was frightened now and for a moment thought that she had better drop the heavy keg and run for her life. But no! That powder was needed to save the lives of the settlers in the fort. They depended on her to get that powder back. The brave girl hugged the keg of powder tighter and sped toward the fort.

One of the Indian warriors was now gaining on her. He raised his war club on high ready to strike her down. Just then a shot rang out from the fort, and the Indian fell dead behind her, but the other savages continued to gain. More shots came from the fort. The Indians slowed down just as Betty reached the gates to the fort, which were hurriedly opened for her to run through.

Colonel Zane, who had been waiting for her with tears in his eyes, grabbed the precious keg of powder as the girl sank to the ground. She was not hurt, but she was exhausted from running.

The men, women, and children within Fort Henry were now safe. The powder was given to the men, who were thus able to hold off all further attacks by the Indians until help arrived from other settlements. Brave Betty Zane had saved the day.

HOW THE BRAVE WOMEN
OUTWITTED THE INDIANS

JEMIMA JOHNSON

You have just read how Betty Zane saved old fort Henry in West Virginia. Another brave girl of the War of Independence was Jemima Johnson. One day in 1782, the people in the fort at Bryan's Station in Kentucky, looked out across the clearing and saw several Indians at the edge of the woods just out of rifle range. They were Wyandottes on the warpath and their faces were smeared with war paint.

"Let us go out to show those Indians that we are not afraid to fight," said one young man.

"No," said Captain Craig who was in charge of the fort and knew all about Indian fighting. "That is just exactly what they want us to do. If we march out of this fort, the main force of the Indians will attack from the rear. I am sure they are out there now hiding in the woods where we cannot see them."

The settlers agreed with Captain Craig and decided to stay inside the fort. But the Indians had come unexpectedly, and there was not enough water for a long siege. There was no spring or well within the fort. All of the water had to come from a spring in front of the fort down where the painted savages could be seen.

Who would go for the water?

Captain Craig called all the settlers together. "I don't like the look of things," he said. "We need water badly. Someone has to go down to the spring to get it. We know that Indians are waiting down there in the woods and there are probably many more at the rear of the fort. Usually the women go down for the water, but it will be dangerous if they go today. Yet if we men go for the water, the Indians will know that we suspect them and will start a fight. If we are surrounded and killed, who will then be left to protect the women and children in the fort?"

Everyone remained silent. They knew that the captain was right.

However, if the women went down to the spring out of range of the guns from the fort, there was very little that could be done to prevent the Indians from capturing them. The women and children would then be taken away and probably tortured or killed. The settlers were afraid to make a decision. No one said a word.

As the settlers looked from one to another to see who would speak first, Jemima Johnson stepped forward. "I am not afraid. Give me the buckets. Let me go for the water." Her husband was away in Virginia and her young son, Richard, was only two years old, but she was not afraid to risk her life to save the settlement.

When the other women heard the brave Jemima offer to go, they said that they would go, too, and take their older children with them to help carry more buckets of water.

Carrying as many empty buckets as they could, the women of Bryan's Station, led by Jemima Johnson, started off for the spring.

If you had seen them that hot afternoon in August, 1782, you would never have thought for a moment that anything was wrong. The women chatted and laughed as they slowly walked down the path to the spring. Although they knew that at any moment the Indians might rush upon them from the woods, they did not show the terror that was in their hearts.

The hidden Indians were surprised that these women and their children were coming down to the spring for water just as they did every day. Surely the men in the fort did not know that the Indians were there ready to attack or they never would have let the women and children leave the fort. The Indian Chief gave the signal to his warriors to stay hidden. If the men did not know that the Indians were there, it would be better to make a surprise attack after dark and capture the fort.

Jemima stood there at the spring keeping a sharp lookout while she laughed and joked with the other women who filled their buckets to the top with the precious water. When all the buckets were filled, the women and children walked slowly back to the fort. Not a shot was fired.

The men who were waiting anxiously behind the stockade, sighed with relief as they swung open the gate to let the

While the women loaded the guns, the men fired upon the savages.

women and children inside the fort. Now they had water enough to withstand an attack.

That night the men were ready when the Indians attacked. While the women loaded the guns, the men fired upon the savages. The Indians were driven back to the woods. Then they fired flaming arrows at the fort, hoping to set it afire. But the older children took some of the water that had been brought into the fort and put out the fires.

All through the night the Indians kept up their attack, but when dawn came they fled away into the forests and did not come back. Bryan's Station was saved by the bravery of Jemima Johnson. Her little son Richard, who was two years old at the time of the attack, lived to become Vice President of the United States fifty-five years later.

CAN YOU ANSWER THESE?

1. What did the Declaration of Independence mean to the United States during the Revolutionary War?

2. When was the Declaration of Independence adopted?

3. When did Congress adopt an American flag?

4. Who made the first American flag?

5. What did the first American flag look like?

6. Who flew the first American flag aboard a U. S. warship?

7. What does each star in the flag represent?

8. How many stars are in the flag today? How many stripes?

9. How did Molly Pitcher get her name?

10. How did Molly Pitcher become famous during the Battle of Monmouth?

11. How did Mrs. Mary Lindley Murray save the American army?

12. How did Betty Zane save old Fort Henry?

13. Imagine you were Betty Zane when the Indians attacked old Fort Henry. Tell what you would have done.

14. Which do you think was the bravest—Molly Pitcher, Betty Zane, or Jemima Johnson?

DO YOU KNOW THE MEANING OF THESE WORDS?

1. alternate
2. anxious
3. artillery
4. blockade
5. decision
6. exhausted
7. barred and bolted
8. favored the British
9. frontier settlements
10. gallant deed
11. Revolutionary War
12. War of Independence
13. mansion
14. precious
15. savages
16. stockade
17. suspect
18. tortured

CAN YOU MATCH THESE?

Match the name of the person in the first column with the correct statement in the second column.

1. Betsy Ross
2. John Paul Jones
3. George Washington
4. General William Howe
5. General Israel Putnam
6. Betty Zane
7. Mary Lindley Murray
8. Jemima Johnson

a. Saved old Fort Henry
b. Made the first American flag
c. Escaped from General Howe
d. Flew the first American flag at sea
e. American Commander in Chief
f. British General who captured New York
g. Saved Bryan's station
h. Saved Putnam's American army

THE BIRD WOMAN
SHOWS THE WAY

SACAGAWEA

(Sar-car-jar-WAY-ar)

In the Indian language *Sacagawea* means *Bird Woman*. If it had not been for the Bird Woman, the first American expedition to the Northwest would probably have perished in the wilderness.

In 1803 President Thomas Jefferson persuaded Congress to purchase the Louisiana Territory from France. This vast tract of land extended from the Mississippi River west to the Rocky Mountains and from Mexico north to Canada. It doubled the size of our nation and was one of the greatest events in the history of the growth of the United States.

At that time very little was known about the territory, so President Jefferson sent out an expedition, headed by Meriwether Lewis and William Clarke, to explore it. They never would have been able to make the trip if it had not been for Sacagawea, who guided them through the wilderness.

Sacagawea was a beautiful Indian princess who grew up in the tepee of her father, one of the chiefs of the Shoshones, or Snake Indians, as they were sometimes called. The Indian village in which she lived was located on the banks of the Snake River in the foothills of the Rocky Mountains in what is now the state of Idaho.

One day when the little girl was about nine years old, the little village of the Shoshones was greatly alarmed to hear the war cry of the Minnetarees. These Indians had been the enemies of the Shoshones for many years. Now the Minnetarees had gathered together a great band of their warriors and had come to seek revenge for previous defeats.

The little village of the Shoshones could not hope to withstand the attack of so many. The Shoshones tried to escape, but many were killed. Their women and children were carried off by the victorious Minnetarees to their lands near where the city of Bismarck, North Dakota, stands today.

There Sacagawea was sold as a slave to a French half-breed, who acted as an interpreter for the fur traders of the Northwest Fur Company. Four years later, when she was 14, he married her. In February of the following year her little son was born. She named him Baptiste.

In the meantime Lewis and Clark had arrived at the village of the Minnetarees and had decided to spend the winter there before pushing on farther west. They traded with the Indians for food and other supplies that they would need.

One day while talking to the French half-breed interpreter, Clark asked him if he knew anyone who could guide them westward through the land of the Sho-shones.

"Sure," he replied in French. "My wife, Sacagawea, is a Shoshone. We will go with you if you wait until after the baby is born."

And so it was in April, two months after the baby was born, that Lewis and Clark started westward. With them went the French half-breed and his young wife, Sacagawea, with her baby strapped to her back.

The 15-year-old Sacagawea carried her little son every foot of the way during the 5,000-mile journey that was to last for a year and a half. Although the trip was

The 15-year-old Sacagawea carried her little son every foot of the way.

hard—sometimes paddling a canoe, sometimes climbing up the mountains, sometimes riding across the prairies or marching through the deep forests, Sacagawea never seemed to tire. The men wondered how this young girl could withstand such hardships. No matter whether it was hot or cold, sunny or rainy, she never complained.

At last came the day when Sacagawea pointed to the hills in the distance. Her eyes seemed to dance with joy. "There is where I used to live," she said. "This is the beautiful land of the Shoshones."

Lewis and Clark were glad to hear this, for they needed horses and guides to make the trip across the mountains. They hoped that the Bird Woman could get the supplies from her tribe.

Fortunately for Lewis and Clark, they found that Sacagawea's own brother was now chief of the tribe. When the two met,

they were overjoyed to see each other alive
and well. Each had thought that the other
had been killed that day six years before
when the Minnetarees had attacked. The
chief was glad to help Sacagawea and her
white friends.

It was a little difficult for Lewis and
Clark to make their needs known to the
chief, for they did not know any of the Indian language. Lewis would speak in English to one of his men who would repeat in
French to Sacagawea's husband what
Lewis had said. Then he, in turn, would
pass the message along to his wife in the
language of the Minnetarees. The Bird
Woman would then translate it to her
brother in the language of the Shoshones.
This took a long time, but often Lewis and
Clark found that it was not necessary to
talk. A few gifts and a sign or two with
the hands served the same purpose.

At first Lewis and Clark were afraid

that Sacagawea would want to stay with her own people and refuse to continue to act as their guide to the Pacific. This would have left them far from home without a guide or interpreter. But Sacagawea remained loyal to the American explorers.

On they went across the Rocky Mountains. Sacagawea showed them how to go so that they would find the stream on the western slope of the mountains that broadened out into a mighty river and at last emptied into the Pacific Ocean itself. They followed trails known only to the Shoshone Indians. Without Sacagawea's help, Lewis and Clark would probably have died amid the snows on the mountains. Her cheerful manner kept the expedition going. The life of everyone depended on her. When supplies ran low, she alone knew which of the wild plants could be eaten to keep the men from starving.

At last in November they arrived at the shores of the Pacific and built log cabins in which to spend the winter.

When spring came, they started back and, in August, arrived at the Minnetaree village from which they had started the year before. Clark offered to take Sacagawea and her husband and baby back East with him, but they preferred to stay with the Indians.

Lewis and Clark sent to Washington an account of their remarkable journey. This report was of great value as it described the country and the Indians living there. It also suggested opportunities for trade and settlement. As a result of this trip the United States laid claim to Oregon.

Sacagawea lived for many years and died in 1871 on an Indian reservation in Wyoming. There she often retold her adventures as the first person to guide the white men across the mountains to the Pacific.

DOLLY MADISON

"There is no time to lose, Mrs. Madison," cried the messenger as he rode up in front of the White House in Washington. "The enemy is nearly here, and they have boasted that they will capture you and the President and take you both back to London in chains."

Dolly Madison did not fear for her own safety, but she did not want any of the national treasures that were kept in the White House to fall into the hands of the enemy. When she and her husband, President James Madison, had come to live in the

106

White House five years before, no one had ever dreamed that the day would come when they would have to flee for their lives to escape capture by an enemy.

Dolly Payne had been born in North Carolina in 1772, but she spent most of her childhood days on a big plantation in Virginia. Her father was a Quaker, yet that did not prevent him from joining the American army and fighting for liberty during the Revolutionary War.

After the war, Mr. Payne sold the plantation and moved his family to Philadelphia, the largest city in America at that time. There were many dances and much entertaining in that city which was then the capital of the United States, but Mr. Payne was a Quaker and did not take part in such frivolous things.

The Quaker girls did not have a very lively time in those days. Dolly's father made her obey the strict rules of the

Quakers. Although Dolly was one of the prettiest girls in town, her father would not let her go to the dances. On Sunday she went to the Friends' meetinghouse where in her plain dress and bonnet she sat on one side of the house with the other women and girls, while the men sat on the opposite side.

One day Mr. Payne told Dolly that John Todd, the rich young Quaker lawyer with whom he did business, had asked for her hand in marriage. Her father thought that it would be a fine match for her, and so she consented. The marriage was announced in the Quaker meetinghouse a few months later.

Dolly and John Todd settled down and lived the simple life of the Quakers for three years. Then, in 1793, a dreadful epidemic of yellow fever broke out in Philadelphia. Dolly and her two children went out into the country to escape the epidemic, but her husband had to remain in Philadelphia to take care of his business. Before he could join his family, he became sick and died.

Dolly was very sad and thought that she would never be happy again. But when the yellow fever epidemic was over and she returned to Philadelphia, she found that she was the center of an admiring group of young men. She was young and beautiful, and her husband had left her enough money so that she now could do whatever she wanted.

One of the men who frequently called to see her was Aaron Burr who, at that time, was a Senator attending the session of Congress that was meeting in Philadelphia. One day he asked if he might bring his friend, James Madison, who was anxious to meet her.

Madison was one of the leaders in Congress and had helped to write the United

States Constitution. Although he was twenty years older than Dolly, she was pleased that he had asked to call. She told Burr that she would be delighted to meet the famous Virginian, James Madison.

Madison was equally delighted to meet the pretty, young widow. It was not long before they fell in love with each other and were married at the home of Dolly's sister in Virginia amid much feasting and merry-making.

At her husband's request, Dolly gave up wearing the simple Quaker gray gown and began to take her place as a leader in society. The parties that Mr. and Mrs. Madison gave became very popular, and everyone looked forward to receiving an invitation.

When Thomas Jefferson was elected President of the United States, he made James Madison his Secretary of State. Jefferson's wife had died, so the President often called upon the attractive and witty Dolly Madison to take charge of the state dinners at the White House. The fame of Dolly Madison as a charming hostess spread rapidly.

James Madison was elected President of the United States to succeed Jefferson. Dolly felt right at home when she moved into the White House. "Everyone loves Dolly Madison," said one of her guests one day. "And Dolly Madison loves everybody," was Mrs. Madison's quick reply.

But it was not all fun in Washington where the capitol was now located. In 1812, war broke out between the United States and England because the British stopped our ships. They took off American sailors and forced them to join the British navy.

The American navy was so small at that time that, although our warships won a number of brilliant victories, they were no match for the mighty British navy. In August, 1814, the British landed an army near Washington. No American army appeared to stop their advance. There was great terror in the capital.

President Madison hurried away to see what could be done to stop the British. "If the British come before I get back," he said to his wife before he left, "don't let the state papers fall into their hands."

Reports came to the White House that the British were advancing and were threatening to burn the capitol. Dolly Madison knew that there was no time to lose. She and the few servants who had not already fled away to safety brought out her trunks, and she began packing them with the nation's most valuable papers.

The sound of the guns could be heard in the distance as the last trunk was packed. Just then a messenger rode up with the alarming news that the British were entering the outskirts of Washington and Mrs. Madison must go at once if she wanted to escape capture. There was no time to lose. He said that Mrs. Madison had better not even think of taking the trunks as they would hinder her escape.

"These trunks contain the nation's most valuable state papers, including the Declaration of Independence. If I go, they go, too," said the brave little Dolly Madison.

The White House guards who were standing nearby knew that Dolly Madison meant what she said and started loading the trunks into her carriage. Then she started to climb in herself. Just then she remembered the famous Gilbert Stuart painting of George Washington that hung in the state dining room.

"Wait a moment," said Mrs. Madison. "We cannot leave that painting to the British." In spite of the pleadings of the guards that there was no time for her to go back now, Dolly Madison jumped down from the carriage and ran up the stairs of the White House.

The picture was fastened to the wall so that she had to cut the picture out of the frame. Then Dolly Madison took the painting out and rolled it up. With the picture safe in her hands, she dashed back to her waiting carriage and drove away just in time.

The British could be seen coming down the road, but Dolly Madison escaped. They did not notice the carriage drive off as they were anxious to loot and burn down the White House and the Capitol.

The war ended the next year, and Washington and the White House were later rebuilt. Because of the bravery of Dolly Madison, the state papers were restored to the nation, and the famous painting of Washington can once more be seen hanging on the walls of the White House.

Dolly Madison had to cut the picture out of the frame.

JANE LONG

In Ponca City, Oklahoma, a statue of a typical pioneer woman plodding along with her young son has been erected in honor of the brave women who helped to settle the West. These women, bringing their children and all their household goods with them, marched side by side with their husbands across the prairies and shared all the dangers and hardships of the pioneer. You will not find the names of these women in the history books, but they were heroines just the same. It was they who established the homes on the frontier and helped to bring peace and prosperity to that great section of our country stretching from the Great Lakes to Mexico.

This is the story of one of those women who helped in the early struggle to free Texas. When the United States purchased the Louisiana Territory from Napoleon in 1803, there was some question as to the western boundary. The Spanish had settled in Mexico and had built missions and small settlements across the Rio Grande in what is now the state of Texas. The boundary lines were not settled until 1819. At that time the United States purchased Florida from Spain and, at the same time, gave up all claims to Texas.

Many Americans did not believe that the Government had any right to sell or exchange Texas, which they claimed belonged to the United States as it was included in the original Louisiana Purchase. In Natchez, Mississippi, an expedition was formed to march into Texas and proclaim that territory as an independent republic. The leader was Dr. James Long, who was only twenty-three years old. Although he was young in years, he was already well-known for his skill and bravery.

Four years before, Dr. Long had fallen in love with Jane Wilkinson. He was only 19 at the time, and she was even still younger. Although her relatives said that they were entirely too young, the couple decided the matter for themselves and were married on May 14, 1815.

When Dr. Long started out for Texas, his wife followed him. It was not easy traveling in those days. Mrs. Long and her two small children floated down the Mississippi in a small boat and then traveled overland on horseback in the midst of a pouring rain to reach her sister's plantation at Alexandria, Louisiana. From there, Jane pushed on to Texas to join her husband, but the hardships of the journey had been too much for the children, and the younger baby died.

At Nacogdoches, Texas was declared a free and independent republic. Dr. Long was chosen as its first President.

Dr. Long knew that he would need a stronger force to hold Texas, so he set out for Galveston in the hope that he could persuade Lafitte to help him. Lafitte was a pirate who had become rich and powerful by capturing and looting Spanish ships. Nevertheless, he had helped Andrew Jackson and the Americans defeat the British in the Battle of New Orleans. Dr. Long hoped that Lafitte would help again, but the pirate refused.

In the meantime, Dr. Long heard that a Spanish army had set out to destroy the new Texas Republic, so he sent back word to his wife to escape to Louisiana.

When Dr. Long returned to Nacog-doches, he found that his men had been defeated, and the inhabitants of the town had fled to the United States. He hurried back to New Orleans to raise another ex-pedition. Mrs. Long joined him there.

Soon Dr. Long was again ready to set out at the head of new forces to win inde-pendence for Texas. This time they sailed to Bolivar Point, on Galveston Bay, where they built a small fort. In July, 1821, Dr. Long and his men left to march westward against the Spanish stronghold at Goliad on the San Antonio River.

Jane Long remained behind in the little fort on Galveston Bay, promising to wait there until her husband returned. The days went by, and no news was heard from Dr. Long. The few soldiers that had been left to guard the fort became frightened. They felt sure that the expedition had failed, and that a strong Spanish force

"You may run away if you want to, but I will remain."

would soon attack the fort. They knew that they could not hold out against such an attack and decided to escape at once to Louisiana. They told Mrs. Long that she would have to leave, too.

"I will not go," said the brave pioneer woman, "for I promised my husband that I would stay here until I heard from him. You may run away if you want to, but I will remain."

Deserted by the soldiers, the young wife, not twenty-one years old, stayed there at the fort with no one except her two young children, one a tiny babe who had been born in the fort, and a loyal Negro girl, Kian, who had promised to stay to help the young mother.

The summer came and went, and still no word from Dr. Long. Mrs. Long and the babies suffered from cold and hunger during the following winter. Their only food for a time was oysters and other shellfish that the faithful Kian got from the bay. Besides, there was constant danger from attacks by pirates and Indians.

Once when a band of savages appeared before the fort, dressed in war paint, and prepared to attack, Jane Long fired the cannon at them. The Indians thought that the soldiers must be still inside and quickly ran away.

In the meantime Dr. Long and his men had captured Goliad. Before he had time to send word back to his wife, however, a large Spanish army surrounded the town and forced the Americans to surrender. Dr. Long was made prisoner. Finally he was permitted to go to Mexico City. There he was treated as an honored guest since Mexico, under the leadership of General Iturbide, had just won its independence from Spain.

Unfortunately, Dr. Long was mysteriously shot and killed by a Mexican soldier.

When the news reached Mrs. Long that her husband was dead, she returned on horseback to Mississippi.

Texas finally gained its independence in 1836. Jane Long went back there to live and stayed for the rest of her life in Texas.

DO YOU KNOW?

1. From what country did the United States purchase the Louisiana Territory? When?

2. Who was the President of the United States at that time?

3. What was the size of the Louisiana Territory?

4. Who was sent out to explore the Louisiana Territory?

5. Whom did they use as a guide?

6. Tell what you know about the Bird Woman.

7. How old was the Bird Woman when she started out as a guide for Lewis and Clark?

8. Why was the Lewis and Clark expedition important?

9. Tell about Dolly Madison's early life.

10. How did she meet James Madison?

11. Tell what you know about the War of 1812.

12. How did Dolly Madison save the nation's valuable state papers and the painting of George Washington?

13. Why did Dr. James Long and his men think Texas should be an independent republic?

14. What happened to Dr. Long's first expedition to free Texas? What happened to the second expedition?

15. What happened to Jane Long in the fort on Galveston Bay?

16. When did Texas gain its independence from Mexico? How?

WHAT DO THESE WORDS MEAN?

Tell what each of these words or group of words means. Use each word in a sentence. If you are not sure of the meaning or the pronunciation of a word, look it up in a dictionary.

1. admiring
2. amid
3. announced
4. constant
5. expedition
6. extended
7. flee
8. half-breed
9. hardships
10. hinder
11. a fine match for her
12. brilliant victories
13. charming hostess
14. dreadful epidemic
15. Friends' meeting-house
16. household goods
17. leader in society
18. merrymaking
19. state papers
20. United States' Constitution
21. looting
22. pioneer
23. pleadings
24. persuaded
25. plodding
26. proclaim
27. prosperity
28. shellfish
29. restored
30. session

126

FLORENCE NIGHTINGALE

Throughout the world today wherever there is war, flood, famine, or other disaster, there you will find Red Cross nurses and helpers bringing care and relief to the wounded and suffering. But it was not always that way.

Less than a hundred years ago, the British were fighting the Russians in the Crimea. The wounded were dying by the hundreds because there was no one to take proper care of them. As one newspaper reporter wrote, "The sick appear to be tended by the sick, and the dying by the dying."

Something had to be done to save the lives of the soldiers. Who would go? There was only one woman in England ready and trained for the work—that was Florence Nightingale. She quickly organized a group of thirty-four nurses and volunteered her services. Many a soldier who was wounded in that war owed his recovery to that wonderful woman.

Florence Nightingale was named after the lovely Italian city of Florence, Italy, where she was born in 1820. Her parents were not Italians. Her father was one of the wealthiest landowners in England, and her mother was the daughter of a member of the British Parliament.

As a young girl, Florence grew up on her father's beautiful estate in England. She was pretty, well educated, and rich. But instead of wishing for luxuries for herself, she thought only of helping others. She wanted to be a nurse.

In those days only girls of the lower class became nurses. It was not thought proper for the daughter of one of the wealthiest men in England to be a nurse. Her father wanted her to be a fine lady and stay at home and entertain like her lovely mother. He did everything he could to persuade his daughter to give up the idea of becoming a nurse.

Her family took her abroad to see the sights, hoping that she would forget about nursing. But wherever she went, she visited the hospitals and asylums to learn how things were being done to care for the sick.

On one of these trips she visited Pastor Fliedner's great Lutheran hospital at Dusseldorf on the Rhine. In addition to the hospital, there was a training school for nurses. Florence Nightingale was so interested in the work that she spent several weeks there. Pastor Fliedner thought that this gentle English lady would quickly give up if she had to do any hard work.

"Your first job will be to scrub the floor," said Pastor Fliedner. Florence Nightingale was not afraid of hard work. She got a pail of water and a brush and began to scrub. When she had finished, the floor had never before been so clean. She completed her course of instruction in nursing with an excellent record. Pastor Fliedner knew that this young woman was meant for nursing.

Back in London she finally won her family's permission to do hospital work. She was appointed manager of the Harley Street Sanitarium. As the first woman manager of a hospital, she had a great responsibility ahead of her. For several years she stayed there giving freely of her time and fortune. Everything was going well at the hospital when reports were printed in the newspapers that British soldiers were dying by the hundreds in the

Crimea because there was no one to take care of the sick and dying.

Finally Mr. William Howard Russell, one of England's well-known war reporters, wrote to his paper in London, "Are there no devoted women in England able and willing to go out to take care of our sick and suffering soldiers in the East? Are none of the daughters of England at this extreme hour of need ready for such a work of mercy?"

As soon as Florence Nightingale heard of this, she wrote to her friend, the British Secretary of War, telling him that she had organized a group of nurses for service and was ready to leave for Scutari in Turkey. "We shall feed and lodge ourselves there," she said, "and be no expense whatever to the country."

The War Department did not approve of a group of female nurses going so far away but at last gave its consent. On October 21, 1854, Florence Nightingale and her band of thirty-four nurses left England for Scutari, which was one of the bases for the wounded men sent back from the fighting in the Crimea.

Upon arriving there, they found conditions very bad. The doctors were overworked. Thousands of soldiers lay sick and dying. The supplies that were needed could not be found.

Florence Nightingale and her nurses set to work at once to put things in order. The mattresses needed washing. The floors needed scrubbing. The men's wounds needed dressing, and there were a thousand and one other things that required attention. The women started in at once washing, cleaning, scrubbing, caring for the wounded, and doing everything possible to relieve the suffering of the men.

The doctors, who had wondered at first of what use these women would be, won-

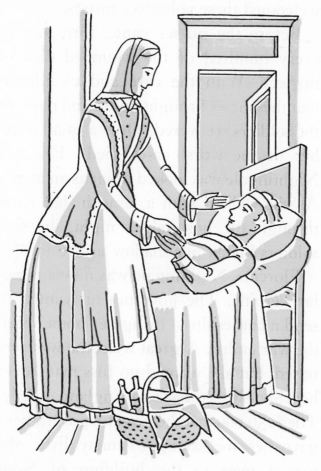

Florence Nightingale set to work at once to put things in order.

dered no more. The wounded soldiers welcomed these volunteer nurses.

Before the nurses came, forty out of every hundred of the wounded died of neglect. With the care and cleanliness that the nurses brought, more and more of the soldiers recovered. Only a small number of the worst cases died. Florence Nightingale was looked upon as an angel. As she walked with a lamp in her hand through the hospital at night, the sick soldiers kissed her shadow as she passed.

Florence Nightingale was now a popular heroine. The government wanted to send a battleship to bring her home when the war ended. A great welcome was prepared, but she wanted no fuss made over her. She slipped back to England quietly. The $250,000 that the grateful government gave her for saving so many lives, she turned over to the building of Saint Thomas Hospital.

Although her war experiences left her in poor health, Florence Nightingale lived for many years until at last, in 1910, she died at the age of 90. In the meantime she was honored by the crowned heads of Great Britain and received many other tributes.

In 1863 the representatives of sixteen countries gathered in a convention at Geneva, Switzerland, at the suggestion of two Swiss gentlemen, Jean Henri Dunant and Gustave Moynier. This convention made it possible to organize the International Red Cross by recognizing the neutrality of those who went out to help the wounded during wartime. The splendid work begun by Florence Nightingale is now carried on throughout the world by millions of persons. The Red Cross lives on as a monument to this very remarkable woman.

THE LADY OF
THE BATTLEFIELDS

CLARA BARTON

Clara Barton was born in Oxford, Massachusetts, on Christmas Day in the year 1821. She was truly a Christmas gift to the nation, for her entire life was devoted to helping others.

Clara Barton's grandfather had fought through the Revolutionary War. Her father had served with General Mad Anthony Wayne in his expedition against the Indians on the western frontier. As a little girl, Clara loved to sit on her father's knee and listen to his stirring stories of battles and dangerous adventures.

Clara's father owned a farm on which he raised fine horses. Her older brother, David, taught her to ride almost before she could walk. David would boost her up on one of the young horses. Then, jumping on the bare back of another, he would go galloping with her around the pasture. It was a good thing that her mother did not see her little daughter on those mad rides. The shock of seeing the tiny girl hanging to the horse's mane while the beast ran at top speed around the pasture might have been too much for the dear old lady.

The little girl was never injured, however. Years afterward, in her *Story of My Childhood,* she wrote, "When I found myself on a strange horse, in a trooper's saddle, flying for my life or liberty in front of pursuit, I blessed those wild gallops among the beautiful colts."

When she was just eleven years old, her

brother David met with a serious accident and for two years was an invalid. Little Clara Barton became his devoted nurse. She carried out the doctor's orders, brought David his medicine, and kept his room clean and tidy. No task was too small, and none too great for the little girl.

In those early days she showed that she was a born nurse. But those two years of giving constant care to her brother kept her from playing with friends of her own age and left her shy and timid.

Her mother was worried about Clara. One day a friend suggested that it would be a good thing if the girl became a teacher. "In helping others, she will forget about herself," said the friend.

Clara Barton was a very bright girl. Her older brothers and sisters taught, so that it was easy for the young girl to get a teaching position in the country school.

Putting up her hair, and lengthening

her skirts, the shy 15-year-old girl stood in front of her class that first day fearful and trembling. "It was one of the most awful moments of my life," said Clara Barton in later years.

She wanted to run away but decided that, since she had accepted the position, she would have to stay and do the best she could. By the end of the first day, her fears had disappeared, and she knew that she would love teaching. For the next ten years she remained as teacher in the small school there at North Oxford.

Clara Barton knew that she needed more education herself. Although there were no women's colleges in those days, she entered the Clinton Liberal Institute in New York State.

When she finished with high honors, she accepted a position as a teacher in New Jersey. She was a success from the beginning.

At that time there were no public schools in that neighborhood, so she decided to organize the first public school in near-by Bordentown. The school opened in an old building with six boys. Within a year, Clara Barton's school had become famous in that part of the state, and it had grown until there were 600 pupils. But she had worked so hard that her health broke down and she had to leave.

Clara Barton then went to Washington, D.C., and secured a position with the Government. She was the very first woman to be employed by the United States Government. Thus it was that Clara Barton was working in Washington when the War between the States broke out.

Among the first Union soldiers to respond to the call for volunteers was the Sixth Regiment from Massachusetts. While passing through Baltimore on its way to protect the capitol at Washington, the regiment was attacked by a furious mob. Many of the soldiers were wounded.

Clara Barton was in the crowd in Washington waiting to greet the soldiers. The tears came to her eyes when she saw that some of the wounded boys were her former pupils from North Oxford. She immediately asked if she could help. When her request was granted, she and her friends began binding up the soldiers' wounds with handkerchiefs or whatever else was handy.

The next day she organized a group to bring food and other comforts to the soldiers who were housed in the Senate. As the men ate, she read to them from a Massachusetts newspaper, *The Worcester Spy*.

The soldiers were so interested in the news from their home state that it gave Clara Barton an idea. She wrote to the newspaper explaining the need of supplies for the Massachusetts Sixth Regiment and said that she would be glad to distribute them. Soon her rooms were overflowing with supplies for the soldiers.

Since the first battles of the war were fought not far from Washington, many wounded soldiers were brought back to that city for medical attention. Clara Barton saw these young men whose wounds had not had proper attention. She realized that if she could have been on the battlefield and attended to their needs before it was too late, many of those who were dying would have had a chance to live. She, therefore, immediately requested permission to go to the fighting front.

At first, she could not obtain the necessary papers giving her the right to go. "Whoever heard of a woman on a battlefield?" she was told. "Don't you know that you may be killed by the guns of the enemy?"

"I am not afraid," replied Clara Barton.

"I am the daughter of a soldier. These brave boys who are fighting for us need my help and the supplies that I can take to them. You must let me go."

Finally she did obtain official permission. She arrived at the battlefield the day after the Battle of Cedar Mountain and brought aid, comfort, food, and medicine to the wounded and the dying. Her hot coffee and soup brought cheer to the soldiers. It made no difference whether a man was from the North or the South. If he needed help, she was there ready and willing to give care and comfort.

Through the next four years of the war, she could be seen near the battlefields of Bull Run, Antietam, Charleston, Richmond and many other places. Wherever there was fighting, there Clara Barton set up her tent and helped to dress the wounds of the soldiers and serve hot food to the hungry.

143

Although she was often in danger, she managed to escape injury herself. On several occasions she missed death by inches. Once as she bent over to give a wounded man a drink, a bullet ripped through the sleeve of her dress and killed the soldier.

When the war was over, many of the soldiers who had started out so bravely failed to return. President Lincoln received hundreds of letters from parents asking what had happened to their sons. Lincoln asked Clara Barton to help trace the 60,000 men that had been reported as missing. For four years she searched the hospitals and prisons and graveyards. She was able to get information about 30,000 of the missing soldiers and notified their parents.

The name of Clara Barton became known throughout the nation, and she was constantly being called upon to speak before many groups about her experiences. Finally, worn out from doing too much work, she was ordered by her doctor to take a trip to Europe for a rest.

While she was stopping at a hotel in Geneva, Switzerland, there was a knock at her door. Representatives of the International Red Cross had come to ask her why the United States had not joined their organization.

"I never heard of the Red Cross," said Clara Barton. "Please come in and tell me about it."

Clara Barton listened to the gentlemen tell how the Red Cross had been formed at Geneva a few years before and how twenty-two nations had already joined. She realized how much good an organization like this could do. She had struggled almost alone through four years of war, saving many lives. If there had been thousands of persons instead of just herself, she knew that many more soldiers could have been saved. She decided then and there she would do everything possible to see that an American Red Cross was organized.

It was a long struggle before she could convince the United States that an American Red Cross was needed. The people here thought that we would never have another war and did not want to get mixed up in foreign wars. But when she reminded them that the Red Cross was needed just as much in peacetime as in war, they began to listen.

In March, 1882, Clara Barton's untiring efforts were successful. The United States signed the treaty and became a member of the International Red Cross Organization. Clara Barton became the first president of the American Red Cross.

Although she was now 61, an age when most people are beginning to think of retiring, she continued in office as president

Clara Barton decided she would do everything possible to see that an American Red Cross was organized.

for nearly a quarter of a century. Under her able leadership, the American Red Cross expanded rapidly.

It was Clara Barton who persuaded the International Red Cross to adopt the American plan so that the organization would be ready, not only to help the wounded in wartime, but also be ready to go at any time to help those who were suffering from floods, famines, earthquakes, storms, plagues, and other disasters.

Clara Barton was small and frail, being only five feet three inches in height, but her fame was great. The name of Clara Barton became known throughout the world, and the American Red Cross, which she founded, has brought relief to countless thousands suffering from floods, fires, famines, wars, and epidemics.

COMPLETE THESE SENTENCES

Complete these sentences by supplying the missing word or words now indicated by a number in parentheses ( ).

1. Florence Nightingale was the daughter of a wealthy (1) land owner.

2. She wanted to be a (2).

3. When the Crimean War broke out, she volunteered to go there to help as a (3).

4. The British were fighting the (4) in the Crimea.

5. Florence Nightingale and the other nurses were able to (5) many lives by giving the wounded soldiers the proper care.

6. Later the International (6) was organized at Geneva to care for wounded soldiers in wartime.

7. Clara Barton was born in (7) in the year 1821.

8. At the age of 15 she became a (8).

9. At the beginning of the War between the States, Clara Barton helped the (9) soldiers.

10. Later she obtained permission to go directly to the (10) to help the soldiers.

11. After the war she helped to trace the 60,000 men who had been reported as (11).

12. On a trip to Europe she heard about the International (12).

13. As a result of her efforts, the American (13) was organized and she became its first president.

WHAT DO THESE WORDS MEAN?

1. appointed
2. asylums
3. colts
4. convince
5. disaster
6. extreme
7. famine
8. fuss
9. grateful
10. greet
11. binding up wounds
12. course of instruction
13. crowned heads of Europe
14. family's permission

15. feed and lodge themselves
16. gave its consent
17. hour of need
18. popular heroine
19. recognizing the neutrality
20. required attention
21. horse's mane
22. lengthening
23. luxuries
24. mercy
25. plagues
26. pursuit
27. relief

WRITE A REPORT ON ONE OF THESE

1. International Red Cross
2. American Red Cross
3. Crimean War

THE SWEDISH NIGHTINGALE

JENNY LIND

More than a hundred years ago, a little girl sat in a window in Stockholm singing to her cat. Just then the maid of Mademoiselle Lundberg, a dancer at the Royal Opera House, passed by and stopped to listen. As a result, the little girl was started on a career that made her one of the most famous singers in the world.

The child's name was Jenny Lind. She was born in Stockholm, Sweden, in 1820. Her father and mother were so poor that they could not take care of their daughter.

When her grandmother went to the Old Widow's Home to live, she took Jenny with her. The little girl was so young at the time that she did not think it was a hardship to live there. At the Home there was a big white cat. Jenny made believe he was a prince that had been changed into a cat by a wicked witch. She hung a blue ribbon around his neck and loved to sit in the window and sing to him.

When Mademoiselle Lundberg's maid heard the little girl singing to the cat, she hurried home and told her mistress that she never before had heard such beautiful singing.

Mademoiselle Lundberg sent for the little girl and was enchanted with her lovely voice. She then arranged to have Jenny Lind sing for Herr Croelius, the Court Secretary and singing master at the Royal Theater. He, in turn, was moved to tears when he heard her sweet voice.

As a result, Jenny Lind was educated and taught to sing at the expense of the

Swedish Government. From the age of 10 she was what was called an "actress pupil," and, from time to time, took part in the plays that were produced at the Royal Theater.

When she was 16, she began to study for the opera. One day she was singing one of the operas for her teacher. When she finished, the teacher said nothing. "What is the matter?" asked the puzzled girl. "Did you not like my singing?"

"You are wonderful," he replied. "I can teach you nothing more."

On March 7, 1838, Jenny Lind, at the age of 18, was given the leading part in an opera. She was a success from the beginning. As she said later, "I got up that morning one creature; I went to bed another creature. I had found my power." It was a great day in the life of Jenny Lind, and ever afterward she celebrated March 7th as a sort of second birthday.

Two years later, she went to Paris to study under Signor Manuel Garcia, the greatest singing master in the world at that time. She had been working so hard and was so excited that, when she went to sing for Garcia, she broke down. The great singing master looked at the frightened girl and said, "Mademoiselle, it would be useless for me to try to teach you. You have no voice left."

Jenny Lind was brokenhearted, but she begged to be given another chance. The great Garcia felt so sorry for her that he told her to give her voice a complete rest for six weeks and then come back again.

Jenny Lind did as she was told. At the end of that time she found that she could sing again, and the famous singing master was willing to teach her. She began to practice the scales and exercises for hours every day.

After a year's hard study under Manuel

Garcia, her wonderful voice had improved greatly. She appeared in opera and in concerts in many parts of Europe where she met with tremendous success. The opera houses where she appeared were always crowded. Many persons had to be turned away because there was no more room.

In 1847 Jenny Lind made her first appearance in England. The rush for tickets to hear her was so great that men were knocked down and women fainted. The Queen of England wanted to shower her with valuable gifts, but she accepted nothing but a bracelet. Two years later, she gave up the opera and devoted herself exclusively to concert singing.

At that time America was developing rapidly, and the people here hoped that the famous "Swedish Nightingale," as she was called, would cross the ocean to sing for them. P. T. Barnum, who later became famous with his circus, offered Jenny Lind one thousand dollars a night if she would come. She finally agreed to appear in 150 concerts in America.

P. T. Barnum had trouble in raising the $150,000 as that was a great deal of money in those days. People told Barnum that he would be ruined as he could not expect to get that amount back. But Barnum was sure that the people of America would come to hear Jenny Lind sing and went right ahead with his plans.

Barnum was right. Crowds of people were at the dock to welcome the Swedish singer to America. Twenty thousand came to her hotel that night to greet her. There was such a demand for tickets for the first concert, which was to be held at Castle Garden in lower New York, September 11, 1850, that the tickets were sold at auction. Some persons paid as high as $650 for a single ticket.

Jenny Lind's share of the proceeds from

Some persons paid as high as $650 to hear Jenny Lind sing.

the first night's concert was not $1,000, as promised, but nearly $10,000. She was so thrilled that she sent for the Mayor of New York and told him to divide the money among the poor of the city.

P. T. Barnum sold over $700,000 worth of tickets to the people of America who came to hear Jenny Lind sing. Of this amount, Jenny received over $176,000. A large part of this she gave to charity. In 1852, at the end of her tour, she married Otto Goldschmidt and went back to Europe to live. Although she never returned to the United States, her fame lives on as one of the greatest singers ever to appear on an American stage.

CHARLOTTE CUSHMAN

If someone were to ask you to name a famous girl or woman, you probably would first think of some movie star or actress. Today her picture may be seen in newspapers and magazines. Whenever she appears in a local theater, crowds of people go there to see her. And yet, will she be famous ten years from now?

How many actresses do you know who were famous ten years ago? The people on the stage or in the movies come and go. Only too often the famous actress of today is forgotten tomorrow, as some new star, who is younger or prettier, takes her place.

But there is one actress who will always remain famous. Of the seven women in America's Hall of Fame, she is the only actress. Her name is Charlotte Saunders Cushman.

Charlotte was born in Boston in 1816. She was a happy child and loved to sing to her dolls as she put them to bed at night. Her little playmates loved her singing, too, and would sit around to listen to her as she pretended to be a famous actress on the stage and sang the songs that were popular at that time.

Her mother and father were very proud of the girl's voice and arranged so that she could take singing lessons. Charlotte studied hard and practiced her singing every day. Soon she began giving singing lessons herself. As she became better known in Boston, she was asked to sing in the church choir and appeared in several concerts. At last her dreams came true and she was given a part to sing in the opera.

At the age of 19, when she was appearing in an opera in New Orleans, her voice failed her. She would never be able to sing in opera again. Things looked very black for the young girl who was just getting started on a brilliant career. Most girls would have given up and gone home and been forgotten.

Charlotte's father had had a good business when the girl was growing up and had been able to provide her with a good education, but his business had failed, and the family was depending on Charlotte to help them. Now that she had strained her voice so that she could no longer sing the high notes, what was she to do?

Charlotte sat in her room crying over her misfortune. What would ever become of her, and what would become of her family? The manager of the theater happened to pass by as she sat crying and asked, "What is the matter?" When Charlotte told him of her troubles, he felt sorry for her and told her that, although she would never be able to sing in the opera again, she might become a great actress if she were willing to study and work hard.

Charlotte thanked him as she dried her tears. "Oh, I am not afraid of hard work. If you will only give me a chance in one of your plays, I know you will never regret it."

The manager knew that Charlotte meant every word she said and would work hard to be a success on the stage. "All right," he replied. "I am planning to produce Shakespeare's *Macbeth* in a little while. If you are willing to study hard for the part, I will give you a chance to be Lady Macbeth."

Charlotte was delighted and the next day began to study for the play. She was young and did not realize that this was a

Charlotte Cushman was a great success as Lady Macbeth.

very difficult part that was usually given only to actresses with a great deal of experience. As she read the lines, she was sure that she could make good. She was determined that she would be a success so that she could earn money to help her family.

Day after day she studied and practiced. When the play opened, she was a great success. In the years that followed she played the part of Lady Macbeth many times, but never with more feeling than that first night when she knew that her entire career depended upon it.

Charlotte appeared for three years at the Bowery Theater in New York which, at that time, was one of the most fashionable theaters in the city. She was popular and great crowds of people came to see her as the star in various plays in which she played the leading parts.

Then one day the theater burned down.

No one was hurt, but all of Charlotte's beautiful costumes were destroyed. The manager who had hired her was left penniless so that Charlotte had to seek elsewhere for employment. It seemed that all the other theaters had plenty of actors and actresses. Things again looked very dark for Charlotte Cushman, but she was not discouraged.

Although there were no parts open for a star such as Charlotte, she heard that she might be able to get a small part at the Park Theater. She was glad to accept any kind of work, so she went there and asked for the position. The manager was glad to have her. She stayed there for three years studying so she would be ready for more important parts if an opportunity arose.

At last the chance came for which she had been waiting. The star of the show in Sir Walter Scott's *Guy Mannering* was taken sick, and the manager of the theater asked Charlotte if she thought she could take the part. Charlotte replied, "I am sure I can. I know the part from beginning to end, and I shall do my very best."

Charlotte Cushman's performance was such a dramatic triumph that the manager said that she could have the star's part as long as she wanted it. From that day her success was certain. For more than thirty years she continued to be America's greatest actress.

WHICH IS THE RIGHT ANSWER?

Choose the right answer to complete these sentences:

1. Jenny Lind was born in
   a. Sweden. b. France. c. the United States.
2. She was taught to sing
   a. by her parents.
   b. by Mademoiselle Lundberg.
   c. at the expense of the Swedish Government.
3. In Europe Jenny Lind was
   a. a great success.
   b. not a success.
   c. not allowed to sing.
4. P. T. Barnum invited Jenny Lind to come to the United States and offered her one thousand dollars a night to sing
   a. in his circus.
   b. in an opera.
   c. at Castle Garden in New York City.
5. After her American concert tour, Jenny Lind
   a. remained in the United States.
   b. never returned to the United States.
   c. returned often to the United States to sing.
6. The only actress whose name is included in America's Hall of Fame is
   a. Jenny Lind.   c. Helen Hayes.
   b. Charlotte Cushman.

167

7. Charlotte Cushman was born in 1816 in
   a. Stockholm. b. Boston. c. New York City.

8. She began her career as
   a. an actress. b. a teacher. c. an opera singer.

9. Charlotte Cushman became an actress
   a. when she strained her voice and could no longer sing.
   b. when she was a small child.
   c. at the age of 19 in New York City.

10. Charlotte Cushman continued on the stage as an actress
    a. for only a short time.
    b. for more than thirty years.
    c. until a few years ago.

DO YOU KNOW THE MEANINGS OF THESE WORDS?

1. career
2. celebrated
3. charity
4. choir
5. concert
6. creature
7. depending on her
8. developing rapidly
9. dramatic triumph
10. her first appearance
11. practice the scales
12. proud of her voice
13. mademoiselle
14. opera
15. penniless
16. performance
17. playmates
18. success

MARY LYON and
ALICE FREEMAN PALMER

Women teachers have always done splendid work in shaping the character of the boys and girls who later, as men and women, made our country the great nation that it is today. Therefore, it is not surprising to find that of the seven women chosen for America's Hall of Fame, five of them were teachers. In this story we shall briefly tell about the lives of two of these famous women: Mary Lyon and Alice Freeman Palmer. To these women, the girls of today owe the opportunity they have for higher education.

Mary Lyon was born on a little farm at Buckland, in western Massachusetts, in 1798—the year that George Washington retired as the first President of the United States. Her father died while she was still a young girl. It was hard work for her mother to take care of the rocky farm, even though her seven children helped all they could.

When Mary was 13, her mother married again and moved to Ohio, but Mary and her only brother remained at Buckland. Her brother ran the farm and paid Mary a dollar a week to keep house for him. The hard-working girl also taught in the little country school for seventy-five cents a week. After six years she had saved enough money to enter Sanderson Academy in Ashfield.

The pupils of Sanderson Academy smiled when they saw the country girl coming to school in a simple, homespun dress pulled together with strings at the neck and waist. They thought that she would not stay very long, but although Mary Lyon did not have much money, she had a brilliant mind. Her classmates did not laugh any longer when they found that the simple little country girl after only one day of study had learned the entire Latin grammar and was able to recite it in class the next day.

Mary Lyon should have gone on to college, but in those days the colleges admitted only men. There was not a college for women in the entire United States.

After studying at Sanderson Academy and Byfield Seminary, she took a position teaching school at Ipswich, Massachusetts. After school hours each day, she went to the home of the Reverend Edward Hitchcock, who later became President of Amherst College. He taught her natural science, while his wife gave her instruction in drawing and painting pretty pictures.

The longer Mary taught, the more she thought how unfair it was that there was no college which would accept the girls after they had finished their studies at an academy. Today there are so many excellent women's colleges that we cannot understand why the people in those days thought it was not ladylike for girls to go to college. When a college for women was suggested, the men just laughed and said that it was not practical.

Mary Lyon was not discouraged. She did not think that a college for women was impossible or ridiculous. A college education would make the girls better teachers and better equip them to make a living or establish a happy home.

Mary Lyon was now over thirty years of age. Although she had worked hard all her life, she had never been able to save very much because of the small salary she had received. But she felt so strongly that a college for women was needed that she gave up her position as a teacher. Traveling by stagecoach, she started out to raise money to build a college for women.

After three years of hard work, traveling from town to town, she had enough money to start building a college at South Hadley in western Massachusetts, ten miles south of Amherst. It had not been easy raising the money. When a person to whom she spoke said that he could not afford to give fifty or a hundred dollars, she said, "I shall be glad to have any gift, no matter how small." The gifts she received varied all the way from six cents to a thousand dollars.

The cornerstone of Mount Holyoke Seminary was laid on October 3, 1836. A year later the college opened its doors to students—the first women's college in America. More than a hundred girls were there to enter. They had come by horse-drawn stagecoaches from all over New England and from four other states as well.

The workmen were still tacking down the carpets and moving the furniture into the four-story main building as the girls arrived. Mary Lyon was there to greet each girl and to invite her to help tidy things up.

From the beginning, Mary Lyon insisted that teachers and students should do all the housework in order to keep down expenses and thus make higher education available to more girls. She also wanted the girls to realize that it was just as important to work with their hands as to work with their heads. In keeping with her ideas of cutting expenses, Mary Lyon would not accept a salary of more than two hundred dollars a year.

During the next twelve years, Mary

The girls had come by horse-drawn stagecoaches from all over New England to enter Mount Holyoke.

Lyon saw her beloved Mount Holyoke grow and expand. The college that had been built to house eighty students had to be enlarged to take care of two hundred and fifty, and as many more had to be turned away each year because there was no room for them.

Under her leadership nearly two thousand young women were educated at Mount Holyoke. Many of them became teachers or missionaries. A short time before her death in 1849 at the age of 52, Mary Lyon said, "There is nothing in the universe that I am afraid of but that I shall not know and do all my duty."

Mary Lyon was a pioneer in higher education for women. Many other colleges for women have followed her plan so that Mount Holyoke and Mary Lyon can truthfully be called the "mother of colleges."

Another famous president of a woman's

college was Alice Freeman Palmer who did so much for Wellesley College in Massachusetts. Alice Freeman was born in 1855 in the little country town of Colesville, New York. She was the eldest of four children—three girls and a boy. Since the Freemans did not have much money, they decided that they could afford to send only their son to college.

One day Alice said to her father, "I want to go to college. I know that there is not very much money in the family, but if you will help pay my way through college, I can get a good position. Then I will help educate my brother and sisters."

Although there were a few colleges, like Mount Holyoke, that were open to girls, most colleges accepted only men. Mr. and Mrs. Freeman tried to discourage Alice from thinking of college, but when they saw how her heart was set on going, they finally consented.

177

The University of Michigan had opened its doors to women two years before. So, in 1872, Alice Freeman enrolled there. To help pay expenses, she taught school part of the day. Although teaching school and attending her college classes took up most of her time, she was able to take part in many of the activities and clubs while at college. In 1876 she was graduated with honors. After graduation from college she taught for a year in Wisconsin and then was principal of a high school in Michigan.

About this time a wealthy lawyer in Boston had opened a college for women on his estate at Wellesley, Massachusetts. It was a beautiful, million-dollar college. All that it needed was good teachers. President Angell of the University of Michigan was asked to help select these teachers. He recommended Alice Freeman.

In 1879, she accepted a position as Head

of the History Department at Wellesley. She was just twenty-four years old. Within two years she had established such a remarkable record for her intelligence and clear thinking that she was chosen head of the college, although at that time she was the youngest professor in service.

Under Alice Freeman's leadership the new college took shape, and Wellesley became known from coast to coast. Miss Freeman took a personal interest in each student. She could recall the names of her students when she met them years later.

In 1887 when she was 32, she married George Herbert Palmer, a professor at Harvard. She resigned as president of Wellesley, but throughout her life she kept up an active interest in the college which she had placed upon such a firm foundation. In letters and lectures and in the books she wrote, she continuously called attention to the advantages girls could gain by going to college to study.

In 1892, soon after Chicago University was founded, Mrs. Palmer was asked to become Dean of Women, and her husband was asked to join the history department there. Although the salary offered was several times a professor's salary at Harvard, Mr. Palmer declined the offer and decided to stay at Harvard. Mrs. Palmer, however, was persuaded to go to Chicago with the understanding that she would not have to stay there more than three months out of the year. She remained there for three years and helped to establish the new college in which both young men and women were enrolled.

When Mrs. Palmer returned East, she helped the poor in the slums of Boston. To the children there she gave these three rules on how to be happy: 1. Every day try to memorize something beautiful that you have read. 2. Every day look for something pretty. 3. Every day do some good deed for somebody else.

Alice Freeman Palmer's own life followed the rules that she recommended to the children of Boston. Thousands were saddened when they heard of the death of this noble woman in 1902 at the age of 47.

EMMA WILLARD
and FRANCES WILLARD

Strange as it may seem, two of the seven women chosen for America's Hall of Fame were named Willard, but they were not related. However, both started out at an early age to teach school.

The first of these women was Mrs. Emma Hart Willard. She was born in Berlin, Connecticut, in 1787, two years before George Washington became the first President of the United States. Her father, Captain Hart, had fought with Washington during the Revolutionary War.

182

Little Emma Hart was a very bright child. She learned to read and write at an early age, even before she entered school. By the time she was 16, she was herself teaching school.

In 1807 she went to Middlebury, Vermont, to take charge of a school for girls. There Doctor Willard met and fell in love with her. In 1809 they were married.

Doctor Willard was very much interested in his wife's idea of a school for the higher education of young women. At that time people believed that an elementary school education was enough for girls. It was thought that if they received a higher education, they would not want to stay home and keep house and make puddings and pies.

At Middlebury there was a college for men, but there was no college for young women. Emma Willard determined to start a school for girls that would have "a grade higher than had ever before been known" in a girls' school. At that time there were no free public high schools, and there was no college for women in the entire United States.

In 1814, Emma Willard opened her school, which was a success from the very beginning. Five years later she published a "plan for improving female education" which suggested that the states should provide for free public high schools.

Today, when there are over three million girls in high schools throughout the United States, it is hard to believe that only a little over a hundred years ago people thought that such an education for girls would be harmful.

Governor De Witt Clinton of New York State read Emma Willard's "Plan" and tried to have the New York State Legislature start such a school. He succeeded in getting the Legislature to grant a charter to Emma Willard so she could establish her school in New York State, but no money was given her to build the school.

The city of Troy, New York, wanted Emma Willard to establish her school there. Although the State of New York would not provide the money, the city of Troy did. The city council raised $4,000 through a special tax and purchased a three-story building with 22 rooms, so in 1821 Emma Willard opened her school in Troy. There were ninety girls from seven states in the first class.

Instead of merely giving the young ladies courses in painting and sewing as was done elsewhere, this school offered courses in mathematics, geography, and history, the same as in the boys' schools. Emma Willard's school was the first in the history of the country to provide this higher education for girls.

Many of the girls who were graduated from her school became teachers. They were the best-trained women teachers of that time. The opening of the Emma Willard School at Troy, which was followed sixteen years later by Mary Lyon's Mount Holyoke Seminary, marked the beginning of secondary and higher education for women in America. The thousands of high schools now throughout the land that are open to girls as well as boys stand as a monument in honor of Emma Willard.

Another remarkable school teacher was Frances Elizabeth Willard who was born in Churchville, New York, in 1839. When she was only two years of age, the family moved to Oberlin, Ohio.

Four years later they started out again in a covered wagon to go to Janesville, Wisconsin, five hundred miles farther west. There Frances was taught at home because there were no schools nearby. It was not until she was twelve that Mr. Willard built a schoolhouse so that his children and the neighbors' children could go to school. When she was 16, Frances Willard was sent to the Milwaukee Female College, and a year later she transferred to the new Northwestern Female College in Evanston, Illinois.

After graduation from Northwestern, she became a teacher in various public schools, academies, and female colleges. In 1871 she became president of the Evanston College for Ladies from which she had been graduated. She was the first woman president of a college in America. When the college was taken over by Northwestern University, she became the first dean of women there but left a few years later.

One day in 1874, she was offered a position as principal of a girls' school at $2,400 a year. She was about to accept it when she received a letter urging her to become president of the Chicago Temperance Union. Although Frances Willard was not rich and needed money to pay her living expenses, she accepted the presidency of the Temperance Union, even though at first she would receive no salary at all. She felt she could do more good in that organization which was trying to improve living conditions throughout the world by preventing the sale of liquor.

Frances Willard had seen the trouble and sorrow caused by heavy drinking and determined that she would devote her life to the fight against it. In 1891, she became president of the national organization, the Women's Christian Temperance Union.

It was hard work. At first she often went without her dinner because she had no money. She would walk long distances in Chicago to speak at meetings because she

Frances Willard made the Temperance Union known throughout the world.

did not have the five cents to pay for car-fare, but she was happy in her work. "Trust in the Lord and do good," her mother told her. Frances Willard managed to keep on with her work until money came in to pay her expenses.

Frances Willard was not afraid of those who laughed at her and the good work that she was doing. She would walk into dirty saloons and there, amid the drunken men, she would drop to her knees on the sawdust floor and pray that these men would realize the evil of their ways and be saved. At first they wanted to throw her out, but there was always someone who would speak up and say, "Oh, let her alone!" As Frances Willard would keep on praying, one by one the men would drop to their knees to pray with her. She had given up her own home in order to rebuild the homes of less fortunate people. "Look for the good in people," said Frances Willard.

Up and down the land she went. Her voice was heard in every city of over 10,000 people. She became famous throughout the country. She made the white ribbon badge of the Temperance Union known throughout the world.

Upon her death in 1898, flags from the Atlantic to the Pacific were flown at half mast in her honor. She is the only woman in America to be honored by having her statue placed in the capitol of the United States at Washington, D.C., and in 1940 she was one of the thirty-five "Famous Americans" to be honored by the United States Government by having her picture placed on a postage stamp.

MARIA MITCHELL

"Twinkle, twinkle, little star,
How I wonder what you are!
Up above the world so high,
Like a diamond in the sky."

How often have we recited that little poem as we looked at the first star of the evening? But most children do not wonder very long. They run off to play or listen to the radio.

Maria Mitchell was different. She wanted to know more about the stars. She studied and read all the books she could about the stars. Then night after night she looked through her telescope at the sky to see if she could find any new stars. She became one of the world's greatest astronomers, and she is honored in America's Hall of Fame.

Maria Mitchell was the third child in a family of ten. She was born on the little island of Nantucket, off the coast of Massachusetts, in the year 1818. Her father was a Quaker and taught school during the day. On clear nights he loved to study the stars through his telescope.

While Maria was still a child, she would often ask her father, "May I look at the stars, too?" Then her father would hold the little girl up and show her how to use the telescope. He was delighted that his daughter took such an interest in the stars that he loved so well.

As the child grew older and was allowed to stay up later at night, she spent more and more time studying the stars.

"If you look long enough, Maria," said her father one day, "I am sure that you will find a new star or even a comet that no one has ever seen before."

"What is a comet?" asked the little girl, who was thrilled to think that someday she might be the one to find a new star.

"The stars do not move, but the comets come and go," replied the father. "We do not see comets very often, as they move around the sun, but you will be able to tell one when you see it. A comet usually appears to have a long, cloudy tail behind it as it travels through the heavens. Many of them are more brilliant and more wonderful than the stars. If you ever discover a new comet, you will become famous."

Night after night Maria Mitchell searched the heavens hoping to discover a new comet. The years went by without success. She was disappointed but not discouraged that she did not find one.

Night after night Maria Mitchell searched the heavens hoping to
discover a new comet.

Night after night Maria kept up her search through her father's telescope. When she was 16, she left school, but she continued to read and study about the stars.

Two years later, when Maria Mitchell was 18, she was offered a position as librarian at the Nantucket Library. There she had more opportunity to read about the stars that she loved so much.

At night she could be seen looking through a telescope at the millions of stars that dotted the heavens. People thought that it was strange that this pretty, young girl should spend her time with a telescope when she could be having more fun at parties. But Maria did not care what others said; she enjoyed looking at the evening sky. She wanted to find a new comet more than anything else.

At last her dreams came true. At half past ten o'clock on the night of October 1,

1847, as she was standing looking through her telescope, there suddenly appeared a speck of light that seemed to be traveling through space with a cloudy tail stretched out behind it. This was something new. She had never before seen anything like it in that location. It must be a new comet.

She rubbed her eyes and looked again. No, it was not a dream. The comet was still there. It was the first time anyone in the world had ever seen this comet.

She called to the others who had already gone to bed. "Come, come quickly! I have discovered a new comet."

Her father rushed to the telescope to see if it was really true. "Yes, Maria, you have discovered a new comet. Now you can claim the gold medal and the money reward that the King of Denmark has offered to the first person to discover a new comet."

Maria Mitchell did receive the grand prize, and her fame was spread throughout the world. She was elected to many important societies and was the first woman to become a member of the American Academy of Arts and Sciences. She also helped to prepare books on astronomy.

In 1865 she was invited to become Professor of Astronomy at Vassar College which had just been established as a college for women. She taught there for twenty-three years inspiring the students with a knowledge and love of the stars. She died in 1889. Sixteen years later she was honored by having her name placed in the American Hall of Fame.

THE GIRL WHO WROTE
A WORLD-FAMOUS BOOK

LOUISA MAY ALCOTT

A little over a hundred years ago a teacher and his wife sat down to supper. Three of his four daughters were there at the table, but where was the oldest, Louisa?

Turning to his youngest daughter, the father said, "May, please call Louisa and tell her that supper is ready."

May ran up to the attic to look for her oldest sister and returned to say that Louisa was busy writing a story and that she could not stop. She did not want any supper anyway.

"Go right back," said her father, "and tell Louisa to march right down here this minute. The story can wait."

The father was a teacher, and there was never much money in the house. Often the girls had to go without things that they wanted. They never thought at that time that someday Louisa would write a story about her family that would become famous throughout the world.

The girls grew up in Concord, Massachusetts, where the family could live at little expense. Louisa loved to write. At the age of 8 she wrote a poem which she called "To a Robin." It was not much of a poem, but her mother encouraged her by saying it was beautiful and that she would keep it always. "Someday you will be a great writer, Louisa," she said. The little girl was very happy as she rushed off to write another poem.

Louisa spent a great deal of time making up stories and telling them to her sisters. She imagined that the little cottage in which she lived was filled with all sorts of exciting adventures. When it rained and the other girls were busy playing, Louisa would hide away in the attic. Sitting there eating apples, she would write her stories.

Her sisters and her friends thought that the stories were wonderful, so that she was encouraged to mail them to the editors of various magazines in the hope that they would be published.

Alas, a few days later, back would come a letter from the magazine with a little note saying: "Your story is being returned as we cannot use it."

Louisa was disappointed. Tears came to her eyes, but each time she would go back again to her attic and write another story. "This one will be better," she said to herself. "I know that they will take this next story."

At last her dream came true. One morning the postman brought her a letter from the editor of *Gleason's Pictorial*. "We are accepting your story for publication. It will appear in the next issue of our magazine. We are enclosing our check for five dollars."

Louisa was so thrilled she could hardly wait for the magazine to be published, but she never told anyone. This would be her secret.

A month or so later she walked into the living room where her sisters were sewing. As she sat down and opened a magazine she was carrying, she tried not to show her excitement.

"What are you reading?" asked her sister Anne.

"Oh, only a story. It isn't very good, but would you like to hear it anyway?"

"Oh, yes," cried her sisters, who always liked to hear Louisa read.

"It says here that the author's name is Louisa May Alcott."

When she had finished, her sisters crowded around her saying, "It's excellent. Who wrote it?"

"It says here that the author's name is *Louisa May Alcott.*"

"Did you really write it?" shouted Anne. "Why didn't you tell us? Oh, Louisa, it's wonderful! Everybody will be talking about it!"

This story started Louisa on a career as a writer. A few months later she wrote *The Rival Prima Donnas.* It was published in the *Boston Saturday Gazette.* This time she received ten dollars and a letter from the editor asking for more stories. Louisa was just 19 years old. She was teaching school to help with the family's expenses, but she dreamed of one day becoming a famous author.

When she was 30, she read in the newspapers of the young men who were fighting in the War between the States. Many were dying of wounds. They needed more nurses, so she gave up her teaching position and became a nurse at one of the hospitals for wounded soldiers. In 1865 her war experiences were published in a book which she wrote called *Hospital Sketches*.

Three years later her father took a number of Louisa's short stories to a publisher in the hope of selling them. The publisher looked them over and shook his head. "These are all right," he said, "but we don't want any more short stories. Can your daughter write us a single long story for girls?" Mr. Alcott was sure that Louisa could.

But Louisa was not so sure as her father. However, she began writing a story of herself and her sisters which she called *Little Women*. The girl who is called Jo in the story is really Louisa, and her three sisters are called Beth, Peg, and Amy. In two months the first part was ready, and her father brought it to the publisher, who was delighted with it. The story first appeared in 1868 and was an immediate success. The second part followed six months later. Louisa May Alcott became famous almost overnight.

Little Women was followed by *Little Men* and other books for which Miss Alcott received over one hundred thousand dollars.

Louisa was a kind and loving daughter. She was glad that she now had enough money to do what she had always desired. She bought all the things for her mother and father and family that they had been forced to do without for so long.

Louisa May Alcott's *Little Women* is one of the best-loved stories for girls. It is still read by thousands of young and old every year. Ask your librarian for it.

LUCRETIA MOTT
ELIZABETH CADY STANTON
and CARRIE CHAPMAN CATT

When the United States Government decided in 1948 to issue a special postage stamp to honor "100 Years of Progress of Women," they searched the records to determine who had done the most to advance the progress of women in the United States. At last they decided on these three women: Lucretia Mott, Elizabeth Cady Stanton, and Carrie Chapman Catt. When the royal purple three-cent stamp appeared, the faces of these three famous women were engraved upon it as a tribute to their work.

Lucretia Mott was born on the quaint island of Nantucket off the coast of Massachusetts in 1793 while George Washington was still holding office as the first President of the United States. Elizabeth Cady Stanton was born in Johnstown, New York, in 1815, when the only means of transportation was by stagecoach or ox cart. Carrie Chapman Catt was born in Ripon, Wisconsin, in 1859. At that time Wisconsin was still a land of giant forests.

These three women, who did so much to help others, came from three different states. Two of them started their careers as school teachers, and all three were active in winning for women the right to vote.

Lucretia Mott was the daughter of Thomas Coffin, a sea captain. When she was 12 years old, the family moved from Nantucket to Boston where she attended the public schools. A year later she was sent to a Quaker boarding school near

Poughkeepsie, New York. At the age of 15 she was made an assistant teacher at that school. Three years later she married James Mott, who was also a teacher at the school.

Lucretia thought it was strange that although the boys and girls were taught the same subjects and had to pay the same tuition at the school, "when they became teachers, women received only half as much as men for their services." She did not think that this was right, and decided that she would devote her life to winning equal rights for women.

When Lucretia married James Mott, they both gave up teaching and moved to Philadelphia. There she began to speak at the Quaker meetings. She took an active part in helping the poor and the oppressed.

Soon her fame as a speaker spread throughout the community. She was sent to a world convention that was being held in London, England. But when she arrived there, she was not allowed to speak before the convention. Only men had that privilege. Lucretia Mott thought that this was very unfair and determined to work harder than ever for equal rights for women.

One of the women she asked to help her was Elizabeth Cady Stanton. Mrs. Stanton was a fellow American visiting in London. She agreed with Mrs. Mott that something should be done to give women the right to vote. Men said that a woman's place was in the home and that she should let the men run the government. But Elizabeth Stanton went right ahead with her plans.

In 1848 she called a Women's Rights Convention at her home in Seneca Falls, New York. Lucretia Mott came to help get things started. It was the first time that anyone had dared to organize such a meet-

In 1848 Elizabeth Stanton called a Women's Rights Convention at her home in Seneca Falls, New York.

ing to demand equal rights for women.

Another woman who attended that convention was Amelia Bloomer who had made a "sensible costume" for herself. The other ladies, fighting for women's rights, liked the outfit so much that they made similar costumes. The men tried to ridicule the women and called the costume "bloomers"—a name which is still used.

In 1865 Elizabeth Stanton was elected the first president of the National Woman's Suffrage Association which had been formed to demand suffrage for women; that is, the right to vote. For the next twenty-eight years she remained as president of the association and spent much of her time traveling up and down throughout the United States, calling upon the women of the nation to arise and fight for their rights.

Carrie Chapman Catt was Superintendent of Schools in Mason City, Iowa, while Elizabeth Stanton was doing her best to arouse the women of the United States to organize and demand the right to vote. Mrs. Catt listened and decided that it was only simple justice that women should have equal rights with men.

In 1890, Carrie Chapman Catt organized the Iowa Woman Suffrage Association and began to lecture throughout that state on the need for women to become interested in better government. She did her work so well that she was asked to help the National Woman's Suffrage Association and in 1904 was elected president.

Under the able leadership of Mrs. Catt, the women of America were beginning to be heard. One state after another began to grant women the right to vote.

The old time politicians objected, for they feared that if women gained this privilege, the former political bosses could no longer maintain control of things. They made fun of the suffragettes and tried to break up their meetings and parades, but the women fought on.

It was not until the end of World War I that the women succeeded in having a resolution adopted by Congress calling for an amendment to the Constitution. This amendment would give women the right to vote in every state of the Union. It was approved by the necessary thirty-six states the following year and became the law of the land. The fight for "Votes for Women" that had been started by Lucretia Mott and Elizabeth Cady Stanton in 1848 and for which thousands of women, like Susan B. Anthony and Carrie Chapman Catt, had worked so hard and so long, had at last been won. Through the efforts of these women, today all women in every state of the Union are guaranteed the right to vote by the nineteenth amendment to the United States Constitution.

TRUE OR FALSE?

*Read each of the sentences and tell which are true
and which are false.*

1. All of the seven women chosen for America's
   Hall of Fame were school teachers.
2. One hundred years ago there were no colleges
   for women in the United States because it was
   thought that such education for girls would be
   harmful.
3. In 1837 Mary Lyon opened Mount Holyoke
   Seminary at South Hadley, Massachusetts. It
   was the first school of higher education for
   women in America.
4. Alice Freeman Palmer at the age of 26 was
   chosen president of the University of Michigan.
5. The city of Troy, New York, provided the
   money so Emma Willard could establish the
   first high school for girls there.
6. Frances Willard devoted her life to the fight
   against excessive drinking of liquor.
7. Maria Mitchell became famous when she discovered a new comet while she was Professor
   of Astronomy at Vassar College.
8. Louisa May Alcott became famous at the age
   of 19 when her novel *Little Women* was published in 1868.

9. The 19th Amendment to the United States, giving women the right to vote, was adopted in 1876.

WHAT DO THESE WORDS MEAN?

1. amendment
2. afford
3. astronomy
4. an association
5. author
6. attic
7. comet
8. female
9. homespun
10. cornerstone
11. maintain control
12. means of transportation
13. as a tribute
14. higher education
15. secondary education
16. shaping the character
17. suffrage for women
18. right to vote
19. women's rights
20. Temperance Union
21. prima donna
22. privilege
23. quaint
24. ridicule
25. seminary
26. telescope
27. suffragette
28. resolution
29. resigned
30. politician

READ

Louisa May Alcott's LITTLE WOMEN

216

JULIETTE GORDON LOW

Although there are now hundreds of thousands of Girl Scouts throughout the United States, it started from a small beginning only about forty years ago. It was due almost entirely to the efforts of one woman—Juliette Gordon Low.

As a child she was known as Daisy Gordon. She was born on Halloween in Savannah, Georgia, just a year before the beginning of the War between the States in which her father served as an officer in the Confederate army. Her family was well-to do, but the war caused many hardships.

Her mother had been born in the North. When General Sherman marched through Georgia and captured Savannah, Daisy was taken to Chicago to live with her grandfather, John Kinzie, who was a government Indian agent. Daisy was thrilled with the Indians who often came and camped near the house. She liked to listen to stories about them and how her own great-grandmother had been stolen by the Indians when she was a small child and kept as a captive for four years.

After the war was over, the Gordon family returned to Savannah where Daisy went to school. After school each day she played with her five brothers and sisters and her many friends. She was always organizing one club or another. Her first club was called "The Helpful Hands." It was a sewing club which she started to give aid and comfort to the world. Her brother did not think much of the club and called it "The Helpless Hands." Perhaps he was right because Daisy could not sew and the club did not last long.

When Daisy was 26, she married a wealthy young Englishman, named William Low. The wedding breakfast was served in the Gordon's beautiful southern mansion. As the wedding couple dashed down the front steps to their carriage which was waiting to start them off on their honeymoon, they were showered with rice by their laughing friends who wanted to wish them good luck.

The next day Daisy's ears began to hurt and she had to return to Savannah to see a doctor. He found that a grain of rice, thrown at the wedding, had gone deep into one of her ears. She had always had trouble with her ears. When the doctor finally got the rice out of her ear, Daisy was totally deaf on that side.

Soon afterward she left for England

where she entered the gay whirl of fashionable English life and was presented to Queen Victoria. Besides a beautiful London house, she had a lovely home in the country and a cottage in Scotland where the Lows used to go to hunt. One day she was out walking in the woods in Scotland when she came to a stream. There was no way to cross the swift-flowing waters except over a fallen log that served as a crude bridge. Daisy was wondering if she should dare to cross the slippery log when a man appeared out of the woods and started to cross the stream.

Daisy ran forward and put her hand on his shoulder to steady herself. The man was so startled that he nearly fell off the bridge. He was about to say something when Daisy said, "It's all right. I am deaf and so my sense of balance is not very good. You go ahead and let me hold on to you so I can steady myself." The man tried to protest, but Daisy pretended she could not hear him, so the man went forward.

When they had crossed the bridge safely, the man turned around. Imagine Daisy's surprise . . . the man was blind.

The happy years passed swiftly. Daisy and her husband traveled to Egypt, to India, and to many other places. But there came a day when Mr. Low was taken sick and died. Daisy had no children of her own. Her life would have been very lonely but fortunately at this time she met Lord Baden-Powell who had organized the Boy Scouts in England. At the first Boy Scout rally in 1909 some girls appeared who called themselves Scouts and who wanted to take part. Lord Baden-Powell decided that it would be better if they had a group of their own and formed the Girl Guides.

Mrs. Low became interested in the Girl Guides and had a troop of her own in Scotland. Then she decided to return to Savannah, Georgia, and organize the Girl Scouts in America. The day she arrived in 1912, she called her friends together and started a troop. It was a small beginning because she had nothing to start with except a Girl Guide handbook and a determination that the young girls of America should have the benefits of a Girl Scout organization.

At that time Juliette Low was 52 and was handicapped by extreme deafness, but she did not let anything stop her in her work. She appointed friends to committees and jobs and told them about it afterward. When they told her they were much too busy to help, she pretended that she could not hear them and smiled saying, "I am glad you will be able to do it."

At first Juliette Low paid all the expenses herself. She was not poor, but neither was she extremely rich. In 1913, Mrs. Low opened a national headquarters in Washington for the Girl Scouts although at that time the organization was still very small. But she was determined that it should grow. In 1914 when more money was needed, she sold her pearls to raise money. "Jewels are not important," she said, "but the Girl Scouts are."

Until 1916, she carried on the work, paid all the bills, and did almost everything herself. These four years were perhaps the happiest years of her life although they were years of hard work. She had always wanted to be of real use in the world, and now she had found the way. At that time the organization had grown so that there were three thousand Girl Scouts. It was too big a job for any one woman to handle alone, and so a National Board was created.

The Girl Scout organization continued to grow. In 1925 Girl Scouts came from all over the world to meet together at Camp Edith Macy not far from New York City. Juliette Low was waiting on the dock in her new uniform to meet and greet these girls and to show them America. Early in January the next year, Mrs. Low came back from a visit to England for the last time. She had been in poor health for some time, but few people knew about it. On January 13 she received a telegram from the National Board. When she tore open the telegram she read these words:

"You are not only the first Girl Scout, but the best Girl Scout of them all."

Tears came to her eyes, for she knew she was dying and would never see her beloved Scouts again. Turning to her maid she said, "Bury this telegram with me."

Four days later she died and was buried in her Girl Scout uniform with the telegram in her pocket. Juliette Low is gone, but the hundreds of thousands of Girl

Under the able leadership of Juliette Low, the Girl Scout
organization continued to grow.

Scouts throughout the nation are a living tribute to the greatness of this woman and her courage and determination that the girls of America should share the benefits of the Girl Scouts' ideals.

JANE ADDAMS

Today when the peoples of the world are trying to find a way to live at peace with one another, it is interesting to read how Jane Addams solved this problem in Chicago. In her search to bring help and comfort to the foreign-born peoples of Chicago's slums, she established Hull House. Here the peoples of all nations came together and worked and played in the American way. Hull House has been a model for other similar places throughout the world.

Jane Addams was born at Cedarville, Illinois, in 1860. Her mother died when Jane was only two years old. Her father was a wealthy man who owned a flour mill in Cedarville. For sixteen years he represented his district in the Illinois State Senate. There he was a friend of Abraham Lincoln.

Jane Addams adored her father. She was a shy and awkward girl who thought he was so grand that he must be ashamed to have a daughter like her. When she went shopping in the stores or to church on Sunday, she would purposely walk with her uncle instead of her father so that people would not know that this handsome man had such a homely child.

One day as she was shopping with her uncle along the main street of the town, her father in his fashionable high hat and fine clothes stepped out of a bank. There, in front of all the people, he took off his hat, and bowing low as if she were a princess, he said, "How do you do, my dear." Jane knew then that her father really loved her and was proud of her. After that she was no longer shy when he was around. Instead, she did everything she could so that he might always be proud of her.

One day while she was driving with her father through the poor part of the town, she saw the small houses that had been built close together and the unhappy look on the faces of the ragged and dirty children who were playing in the streets.

"Why do the comfortable and happy people live over on the other side of the town all by themselves?" she asked her father. "When I grow up, I shall have a big house, but it is not going to be set apart with all the other big homes. It is going to be here among these little houses. Perhaps I can bring some happiness to these poor people."

When Jane was 17, she entered Rockford College in Illinois. When she was graduated, she decided to become a doctor and entered the Woman's Medical College in Philadelphia. But she stayed only a year, having to leave because of trouble with her spine from which she had suffered since she was a child. Her doctor suggested she go to Europe for a rest.

One Saturday night as she rode through the slums of London on the top of a bus, she saw the poor people in their rags buying rotten vegetables which were all they could afford. She never forgot the sight of one poor man who bought a filthy head of cabbage for two pennies and sat there in the street eating it raw. Jane Addams decided that she would devote her life to bringing health and happiness to the poor.

She returned to Chicago and looked for a big house in the slums where she could live and make life more comfortable for the hundreds of thousands of people of all races, colors, and creeds who lived in that crowded area.

At last she found a big house on South Halsted Street. She rented the place and called it *Hull House* for the man who had built it more than 30 years before. Since then the neighborhood had changed, and the house was being used by a factory.

Jane Addams and her friend Ellen Gates Starr had the house repaired. Then they decorated it and put in chairs and tables and other furniture. They put pictures on the walls and hung curtains at the windows so that Hull House should be as attractive and comfortable as possible.

Jane Addams opened Hull House for all the neighborhood to enjoy. On one side lived a colony of ten thousand Italians. On the other side were as many Germans. Poles and Russians lived on the side streets. Further south was a large Bohemian colony. To the north was an Irish colony, and to the northwest there were many Canadian French.

At first this foreign population, many of whom were living in dirty, cold water flats, did not accept the welcome from the "strange American women." No one had ever been so kind to them before. Perhaps there was some trick; so they stayed away.

But gradually one and then another called at Hull House to see what was there. Quickly the news spread throughout the neighborhood that Miss Addams was really very nice—almost as nice as a poor woman.

Soon the Italians, the Irish, and the other people of the neighborhood were dropping in for help and advice. It was not long before the mothers were leaving their babies there while they went to work. A kindergarten was started for the children who were a little older, and hot lunches were served. A few cents was charged for each service so that the people would feel that they were really paying for what they got.

At Hull House the peoples of all nations united into one big
happy family.

Hull House soon proved too small for the needs of the people, and new buildings were added; such as a gym for basketball and dancing, a clubhouse for boys and girls, and several more buildings for other purposes. Here amid pleasant surroundings, the Italians, the Germans, the Russians, and the others forgot their differences and joined together to help one another live happier lives. The peoples of all nations united into one big happy family.

Is it any wonder that Jane Addams felt that the nations of the world should forget their differences, too, and live in peace with one another? She formed the American Women's Peace Party. After World War I she joined the International Committee of Women for Permanent Peace and became its chairman. She took a leading part in the Peace Conventions at The Hague in 1915, at Zurich in 1919, and at Vienna in 1921. "The dictators of the world will make you fight," she said, "but the women of the world will make you free."

In 1931 her many years spent in working for peace were rewarded. In that year the Nobel Prize, which is given to the person who has done most to promote peace throughout the world, was given to her and to Nicholas Murray Butler, president of Columbia University.

Jane Addams' share of the prize was about sixteen thousand dollars. Instead of keeping it, she gave the money to the Women's International League. "The real cause of war is misunderstanding," she said. "Let this money be spent in the cause of international understanding."

Jane Addams died in 1935, but the splendid work that she did for others and her efforts to establish international good will have inspired others to continue to work for permanent world peace.

THE GIRL WHO
COULD NOT SEE, HEAR OR SPEAK

HELEN KELLER

How thankful we should be that we are able to see, able to hear, and able to speak. Just imagine how it would be if you were blind and could not see all the beauty there is in this world of ours. Suppose you could not hear anything that was said to you. That would be bad indeed.

This is the story of Helen Keller, who could neither see nor hear from the time she was a baby, so that for many years she did not even learn to talk. Yet this brilliant girl was able to overcome all these handicaps, to be graduated from college with high honors, and become a useful citizen.

Helen Adams Keller was born in Tuscumbia, Alabama, in 1880. Her father had been a captain in the Confederate Army in the War between the States, and had later become editor of a paper. The home in which she was born was called Ivy Green for the beautiful English ivy which covered the house. In the lovely garden nearby were roses, lilies, and other beautiful flowers.

There was nothing wrong with Helen Keller when she was born. Her father and mother were very proud of their pretty baby as she lay in her crib and, looking up at them, tried to say "pa-pa" and "ma-ma." Her parents looked forward to the time when their pretty daughter would be going to school with the other children of the neighborhood and running home afterward to tell them all that she had seen and heard in the classroom.

For nineteen months Helen grew bigger and stronger. She was able to walk when she was a year old, and she was even able to say a few words. But one day the child refused to eat her breakfast and started to cry when her mother tried to make her eat her cereal. Then the mother felt the child's head and knew that the little girl was sick with a high fever. She put the child to bed and called the doctor.

For days the child lay ill. At last she began to get better, and her parents were happy once more. But their happiness did not last long, for they soon discovered that their darling little Helen would never again be able to see or hear.

The little child was now doomed to a life of silence and darkness. She could not hear what was said to her and did not know how to talk, so she was unable to play with the other children. Is it any wonder that she felt different and would often kick and scream to attract attention? By the time she was 6 years old, her parents realized that something would have to be done for the unfortunate child.

Helen Keller was taken to Baltimore to a famous doctor to find out if he could do something to make her hear and see again, but the doctor could do nothing. The child was hopelessly deaf. However, he told her parents that perhaps Dr. Alexander Graham Bell in Washington might be able to help the little girl. Dr. Bell, the inventor of the telephone, had worked with the deaf for many years.

Dr. Bell looked at Helen and shook his head. "I am sorry," he said. "There is nothing that can be done to make the little girl hear or see, but I suggest that you write to the Perkins Institution for the Blind in Boston and ask if they can send someone to help the child."

It was a wonderful day for Helen Keller when Anne Sullivan arrived in Tuscumbia in March, 1887, to take charge educating the child who could not see or hear and, at that time, could not even speak.

Helen Keller was nearly seven years old. Anne Sullivan was just twenty. From the first day they became good friends. For the next fifty years, until Anne Sullivan died in 1936, they were close companions. It was due to the patience and skill of Anne Sullivan that Helen Keller developed into one of the most remarkable women of our time.

Suppose you had been Anne Sullivan on that day when she met Helen for the first time. What would you have done? How would you have tried to make the child understand what you wanted to say to her?

Anne Sullivan found a way to make herself understood. She gave the child a doll, and, taking Helen Keller's hand, she slowly spelled out "d-o-l-l." The child did

This was the beginning of a new world for Helen Keller.

not at first know that things had names, but she thought that this finger play was fun and repeated it back into the hand of her teacher. This was the beginning of a new world for Helen Keller.

When Miss Sullivan later spelled into the little girl's hand the word "w-a-t-e-r," and then let the water from the pump run over her hand, a new light seemed to brighten the face of the child. Helen Keller knew then that her teacher was trying to tell her the name of the fresh cool water that poured over her hand.

It was now a race for Helen to learn the names of all the things that she had known before only through the sense of touch. During the next three months, she learned almost 300 words and could even put some of them into sentences. Helen Keller wanted to make up for lost time.

Miss Sullivan loved her pupil who was so quick to learn. She lived with Helen, played with her, and worked with her every hour of the day. It would take too long to trace every step in the education of Helen Keller as she grew from a child to a lovely young lady. By means of the hand language, Helen and her teacher were able to talk to each other. It was not long before she was learning and reciting her lessons almost as well as a normal child in school.

Helen learned to read books that had been printed for the blind with raised letters. She also learned to use the typewriter to write what she wanted to say, although she could not read what she had written. That did not matter, however, for she soon was typing without making any errors. By this time she also was able to go on a vacation trip, to swim, to ride a pony, and to do many of the other things that any other child might do.

When she was 10 years old, she heard

about a girl in Norway who was blind and deaf, just as she was, and this girl had learned to speak. Helen was determined that she would learn to speak, too. She finally did learn by feeling the tongue and lips of someone who was speaking.

At first she learned only the sounds of the letters of the alphabet, but soon she was able to say words, and then sentences. In the story of her life Helen Keller writes, "I shall never forget the surprise and delight I felt when I uttered my first connected sentence, 'It is warm.' . . . No deaf child can forget the thrill of surprise, the joy of discovery which came over him when he uttered his first word."

At first she had difficulty with her speech, but Anne Sullivan understood what she was trying to say. Helen practiced speaking day after day until at last she developed a clear voice. Later she was able to speak before large crowds which came to hear her whenever she lectured.

For two years she studied in a school for the deaf, and then, when she was 16, she entered the Cambridge School for Young Ladies in preparation for entering Radcliffe College. There were not many books printed in raised type that she could use in studying her lessons, but it did not matter. Miss Sullivan spelled into her hand everything that the teachers said. Helen took her final examinations in a separate room so that she could use a typewriter to answer the questions.

At the age of twenty Helen Keller passed all the difficult entrance examinations to Radcliffe College, which were the same as those given to the young men entering Harvard College. It was suggested that she take a special course at Radcliffe because she was deaf and blind, but she decided to take the same course as the young ladies who could see and hear.

All through college she had at her side her beloved Miss Sullivan, who never grew tired of spelling into her hand what was said by the teacher. Helen did extremely well in her classes and was able to keep up with the other students.

One of Helen Keller's professors was so pleased with the things that she wrote for her English classes that he suggested she write the story of her life. Helen did write *The Story of My Life* while she was in college. It was such a cheerful, inspiring account of how this young girl was able to live a happy, useful life in spite of terrible handicaps that the *Ladies' Home Journal* published it. So many people wrote in to the magazine praising the story that it was later published as a separate book. With the money she received from her writings, she bought a farm in Massachusetts, and there she lived with Anne Sullivan.

In her writings and lectures Helen Keller did everything possible to help and encourage others who were blind. In 1931 she was awarded a prize of $5,000 by *Pictorial Review* for helping to raise a million dollars for the American Foundation for the Blind. Miss Keller accepted the prize, but she turned around and gave it to the Foundation because she thought that that organization needed the money more than she did. In 1941 the International Federation of Women's Clubs gave her a scroll of honor for her pioneer work in the relief of the handicapped.

The life of Helen Keller is the inspiring story of a woman who has done much for herself and for others to live a happy and useful life in spite of terrible handicaps. As she wrote, "I believe that God wills to make the world better, and I am trying to do my bit to help, and wishing that it were more."

MADAME MARIE CURIE

The sun seemed to shine brighter that morning as a young girl left the hospital and walked down the front steps.

"Am I really cured, mother?" asked the little girl.

"Yes, dear," replied the mother. "With the aid of that radium you are completely cured of cancer. Now you can go out to play and do all the things that the other girls do."

"Thank Heaven for radium," said the girl as tears of joy filled her eyes. "Radium is certainly wonderful if a little tube of it can cure me and thousands of others who are suffering from cancer. Who discovered radium?"

248

"Madame Marie Curie and her husband, Pierre, discovered radium," replied the mother. "It is wonderful, for it has saved thousands of lives."

Madame Curie was born in Warsaw, Poland, in 1867. Her name was Marie Sklodowska. Her mother died while she was still a child, so she was brought up by her father, who was a teacher of physics and mathematics.

Six years before Marie was born, Warsaw had been taken over by the Russians. Only the Russian language was taught in the schools, and the Polish people were no longer allowed to talk of the good old days when Poland had a government of its own.

At a time when most girls are playing with their dolls, Marie was helping her father with his experiments. Each day after school was over, she would hurry back to her father's workshop where she loved to dream of new discoveries.

When she was sixteen, she was graduated from a Junior College with high honors. She had hoped to teach in the schools of Warsaw, but since there were no positions open, she became a governess for a Russian nobleman's daughters.

After several years she returned to Warsaw. She wanted to obtain a better education, so she went to Paris to enter the university. There she could study chemistry. But she needed money to live in Paris, so she looked for work in a laboratory.

Day after day she called on the various scientists. Everywhere she went, she was told, "Science is a man's work. A laboratory is no place for a woman. Why don't you try housework or making hats?"

Marie was determined that she would find work in a laboratory and continued her search. At last she was successful. Professor Gabriel Lippman, who worked in the Research Laboratories at the Sorbonne University, felt sorry for the girl. He told her that he would give her a chance. He wanted to see what she could do.

Marie started at once to clean the laboratory and wash and scour the utensils. The professor was delighted with the result and soon had her helping him with some of his experiments. At the same time, she studied chemistry at the university from which she was graduated two years later with high honors.

Marie became great friends with one of Lippman's students, named Pierre Curie. One day while they were alone together, he turned to her and said, "I love you. We both like to work here in the laboratory. Together we could do great things. Will you marry me?" Marie was so surprised that she hardly knew what to say, but she turned to him and whispered, "Yes, Pierre." They were married soon after.

Marie and Pierre were very happy. They continued to work together in the laboratory. At that time Professor Henry Becquerel had discovered that uranium gave off special rays like rays of light. The Curies were interested to find out more about these rays and what caused them.

Uranium, which was later used in making the atom bomb, was made from a mineral called pitchblende. The Curies spent days and days experimenting with that material. At last, in 1898, their toil was rewarded. They obtained a coarse, grayish salt which they called radium. It was many million times more powerful than uranium in giving off those strange rays which produced various chemical changes. Later research proved it could be used to cure cancer and other diseases.

The discoveries of the Curies brought them world fame. In 1903 they shared with Professor Becquerel the Nobel Prize of

Marie Curie wondered if she could succeed.

$40,000 for the greatest contribution to science.

The Sorbonne University planned to build a new laboratory for Pierre Curie, but he never lived to enjoy it. Before it could be built, he was killed by a motor truck while crossing a street.

Marie Curie was heartbroken. She felt that this was the end of everything. She did not feel like continuing the experiments on which she and her husband had worked so long together.

Then she was offered the position which Pierre had held at the university. She knew that he would have wanted her to continue this work, but no woman had ever held such a position before. Marie wondered if she could succeed, but at last she accepted. She was a success as a teacher from the very beginning. In addition, she continued her work in the laboratory.

In 1911, Madame Curie received the

Nobel Prize again—the only person in the world ever to receive it twice. This time it was awarded to her for her great work in the preparation of pure radium.

Before she died in 1934, she was asked how she was able to gain such great success. She replied, "My success is due to my father, who taught me to wonder and to test; to my husband, who understood and encouraged me; and to my children, who questioned me."

AMELIA EARHART

Today giant airliners are daily winging their way across the United States on regular flights, carrying thousands of men, women and children, as well as mail and express. People are not worried about getting aboard one of the big transatlantic planes for a flight to England or the European continent. The airlines have established such an excellent record for safety that we are apt to forget that flying was considered dangerous only a few years ago.

Twenty-five years ago there were no regular passenger planes making these trips. Many pilots lost their lives attempting to make the dangerous flight across the ocean. The planes in those days were small and depended on their one engine.

Charles Lindbergh astounded the world and won a prize of $25,000 by making the first transatlantic flight in 1927. He was acclaimed one of the most daring men of the age.

The next year a young woman flew across the Atlantic Ocean. She was the first woman ever to attempt this dangerous flight. The newspapers throughout the world spread her name on the front page. Amelia Earhart became famous overnight.

Amelia became used to going places in a great hurry when she was a small child. Her father was a lawyer who moved his family from one town to another every few months, and who took long railroad trips in between times. Amelia liked to go with him on his trips, but she always wished the train would move faster.

Miss Earhart was born in Atchinson, Kansas, on July 24, 1898, but her family moved on almost before she learned to walk. After graduation from high school, she attended several colleges, including Columbia University. During the first World War she worked as a nurse in Canada.

When she was not taking care of wounded soldiers at a Toronto hospital, the girl spent her time watching the Canadian planes in which pilots were training for war service overseas. They went so fast and flew so high! If she could just ride in one of the planes, she knew she could really see the mountains, lakes, and rivers which she loved so well.

After the war ended, Amelia decided to go to California and learn to fly. Her father did not want her to do this. In those days airplanes were considered dangerous. They were made out of wood instead of metal. Their wings were covered with cloth, and their single engine often stopped or caught fire in mid-air. Is it any wonder that Mr. Earhart refused to give his daughter money to go to flying school?

Amelia had a mind of her own, and she knew what she wanted. She sold her fur coat and a few pieces of jewelry to pay her tuition. The school where she enrolled was run by a young man named Frank Hawks, who later became a famous speed pilot.

The serious, quiet girl studied hard and was graduated with honors. Then she started looking for a job as a pilot. She could not find one. There were no airlines in those early days. There were no air mail routes and very few private planes. On the other hand, there were plenty of returned war fliers looking for work. Nobody wanted a woman at the controls of his plane.

Sad but not discouraged, Amelia finally

went back to Boston. There she lived with her mother and became a social worker. She worked hard at her new career, saved her money—and spent most of it taking more flying lessons at near-by Squantum Field. This was just after Charles Lindbergh had flown to Paris, and everybody had become interested in long-distance flights.

At Squantum Field, Miss Earhart became acquainted with Pilot Wilmer Stutz and Louis Gordon, his mechanic. They were planning another transatlantic hop, and they invited her to go along.

Early one morning they sent their big three-motored Fokker plane roaring into the air and headed for Newfoundland. They were grounded there for two weeks by a dense fog. They departed on June 21, 1928, crossed the Atlantic, and landed in Wales twenty hours and forty minutes later.

The English newspapers acclaimed Amelia Earhart as the first woman to fly the Atlantic. She refused to take any of the credit. "I was just a passenger," she said. "Wait till I come across alone before you make a heroine out of me."

She had become famous, however, in spite of herself. When she came back to the United States, she was hired as aviation editor of a big magazine. George Putnam, the publisher, asked her to write a book about her flight. While he was helping her prepare it, Putnam fell in love with the charming author. They were married in 1931.

Amelia Earhart Putnam went right ahead with her new career. She entered the National Air Races and became the first woman to fly from the East Coast to California and back. She was the first woman to pilot an autogiro, and she took the strange new windmill of a plane to a record height of 18,415 feet. She taught many other girls how to fly.

One day Amelia timidly asked her husband if he would let her cross the Atlantic alone. She remembered how her father had forbidden her to learn to fly. Maybe she was afraid that Putnam would say, "No." Instead, he told her to go right ahead, bought her a new Lockheed Vega monoplane for the trip, and went with her as far as Newfoundland.

Amelia took off alone on May 19, 1932. She was the first woman to try this dangerous flight. Soon she ran into fog and rain. Then one of her engines caught on fire. She kept right on going. Fourteen hours and fifty-four minutes after she had left Newfoundland, she landed safely in Ireland. The first thing she did was to call her husband on the transatlantic telephone.

"Well, George, I did it," she told him quietly.

Amelia Earhart was the first woman to fly the Atlantic Ocean.

This time she did not object when London gave her a royal welcome. She danced with the Prince of Wales. She went to Paris and was decorated with the Cross of the Legion of Honor. She received the gold medal of the National Geographic Society. The United States Government gave her the Distinguished Flying Cross. Belgium, Rumania, and other countries also gave her decorations. Back in New York she rode down Broadway while millions cheered, and other people in skyscraper windows showered her with ticker tape.

Most people would have thought that their life work was complete after such an achievement. Amelia was different. She was interested in doing everything possible to develop aviation and to get more people to fly. The way to do these things, she felt, was to make longer and faster flights, and to teach others how to be pilots.

In 1935 she made the first solo flight ever made from Hawaii to California, covering the 2,408 miles in 18 hours and 16 minutes. Later the same year she flashed from Mexico City to Newark, New Jersey, in 14 hours, 18 minutes and 30 seconds.

Then she became a teacher at Purdue University's aviation school. The University and her friends in the airplane industry were so grateful for the work she did there that they presented her with another new plane. It was a Lockheed Electra, and it was equipped with all the very latest flying and navigation instruments. She called it her "flying laboratory."

Amelia decided that this was just the ship she had been waiting for in which to make a trip around the world. She hired Lieutenant Commander Fred Noonan as navigator and co-pilot. On June 1, 1937, they took off from Miami in their "flying laboratory" on what was to have been

Amelia's greatest adventure — a flight around the world.

The travelers did not try to set any speed records. They took their time. They drew many maps and made weather observations which they knew would be useful to other fliers. They stopped at Puerto Rico, Venezuela, and Brazil. They crossed the South Atlantic to Senegal in French West Africa and went on to Egypt and India.

They ran into a severe storm, called a monsoon, on the way to Thailand (Siam) and had to land in Burma. Finally they reached Thailand by way of Rangoon. Then they stopped in the Netherlands East Indies, Australia, and New Guinea. On July 1, just a month after leaving Miami, Miss Earhart and Lieutenant Commander Noonan took off across the lonely Pacific on the most dangerous leg of their trip. It was a 2,556-mile jump to tiny Howland Island.

Then something terrible happened! On July 2, Coast Guard and Navy radio stations picked up a frantic message from Amelia. It said she was lost! The "flying laboratory" was somewhere out of sight of land and was running out of gasoline.

Again the name of Amelia Earhart appeared on the front pages of every newspaper. American warships, which had been standing by in case of trouble, went tearing across the rolling, empty seas in search of the lost plane. The aircraft carrier *U.S.S. Lexington* joined in the hunt. The *Lexington's* planes scouted thousands of square miles. They found nothing, although several radio operators said they had heard weak messages from the missing fliers which indicated that they might have reached land.

The search went on for months under the personal direction of George Putnam. He believed that his wife had reached some tiny, uncharted island and was a castaway. But nothing was ever heard of her again.

WRITE A STORY

Write a story about a girl who became famous in spite of severe handicaps, such as Charlotte Cushman who wanted to be an opera singer but who had to give up when she strained her voice, Mary Lyon who raised the money to build the first woman's college even though most people of that time did not think that girls should be given higher education, or Helen Keller who was blind and deaf and for many years could not even speak.

WHAT DO THESE WORDS MEAN?

Tell what each of these words or group of words means. Use each word in a sentence. If you are not sure of the meaning or the pronunciation of a word, look it up in a dictionary.

1. acclaimed
2. attractive
3. autogiro
4. awarded
5. creed
6. doomed
7. filthy
8. governess
9. handicaps
10. hired
11. aircraft carrier
12. atom bomb
13. a royal welcome
14. Federation of Women's Clubs
15. Girl Guides Handbook
16. Foundation for the Blind
17. refused to take credit

269

18. research laboratories
19. presented to Queen Victoria
20. weather observations
21. monsoon
22. navigator
23. patience
24. physics
25. pitchblende
26. radium
27. slums
28. scientists
29. uttered
30. uranium

WHICH DO YOU THINK?

Which of the girls or women about whom you have read in this book do you think

a. was the bravest?
b. overcame the greatest handicaps?
c. helped others the most?
d. had the most power over others?
e. was the best singer?
f. was the greatest actress?
g. was the best author?
h. was the best flyer?
i. was the best scientist?